ISBN 978-1-5282-8639-8
PIBN 10926220

Forgotten Books is a registered trademark of FB &c Ltd.
Copyright © 2018 FB &c Ltd.
FB &c Ltd, Dalton House, 60 Windsor Avenue, London, SW19 2RR.
Company number 08720141. Registered in England and Wales.

For support please visit www.forgottenbooks.com

1 MONTH OF
FREE
READING

at
www.ForgottenBooks.com

By purchasing this book you are eligible for one month membership to ForgottenBooks.com, giving you unlimited access to our entire collection of over 1,000,000 titles via our web site and mobile apps.

To claim your free month visit:
www.forgottenbooks.com/free926220

English
Français
Deutsche
Italiano
Español
Português

www.forgottenbooks.com

Mythology Photography **Fiction**
Fishing Christianity **Art** Cooking
Essays Buddhism Freemasonry
Medicine **Biology** Music **Ancient
Egypt** Evolution Carpentry Physics
Dance Geology **Mathematics** Fitness
Shakespeare **Folklore** Yoga Marketing
Confidence Immortality Biographies
Poetry **Psychology** Witchcraft
Electronics Chemistry History **Law**
Accounting **Philosophy** Anthropology
Alchemy Drama Quantum Mechanics
Atheism Sexual Health **Ancient History**
Entrepreneurship Languages Sport
Paleontology Needlework Islam
Metaphysics Investment Archaeology
Parenting Statistics Criminology
Motivational

POPULAR GOVERNMENT / Published by the Institute of Government

DIRECTOR, John L. Sanders
ASSOCIATE DIRECTOR, Milton S. Heath, Jr.
EDITOR, Elmer R. Oettinger
ASSOCIATE EDITOR, Margaret Taylor

STAFF: Rebecca S. Ballentine, William A. Campbell, George M. Cleland, Michael Crowell, Joseph S. Ferrell, Douglas R. Gill, Philip P. Green, Jr., Donald B. Hayman, C. E. Hinsdale, S. Kenneth Howard, Dorothy J. Kiester, David M. Lawrence, Henry W. Lewis, Ben F. Loeb, Jr., Richard R. McMahon, Robert E. Phay, Robert E. Stipe, Mason P. Thomas, Jr., H. Rutherford Turnbull, III, Philip T. Vance, David G. Warren, L. Poindexter Watts, Warren Jake Wicker.

Contents

This month's cover photo shows the Charlotte-Mecklenburg Charter Commission convened for an early morning working session. Commission members often met for breakfast at 7 a.m. and worked until 10. See the story on page 26 concerning the proposed consolidation of the governments of Charlotte and Mecklenburg County.

VOLUME 37   MARCH 1971   NUMBER 6

Published monthly except January, July, and August by the Institute of Government, the University of North Carolina at Chapel Hill. Change of Address, editorial business, and advertising address: Box 990, Chapel Hill, N. C. 27514. Subscription; per year, $3.00; single copy, 35 cents. Advertising rates furnished on request. Second-class postage paid at Chapel Hill, N. C. The material printed herein may be quoted provided that proper credit is given to POPULAR GOVERNMENT.

Health Care-

problems and perspectives

By C. Arden Miller

WE HEAR A GOOD DEAL these days about the crisis in health care, and there is indeed a crisis. But precisely what is the problem? What is it that disturbs all of us involved in health education and health services? And what is it in this area that may disturb the 1971 General Assembly? Perhaps some data on the nation's health will help put the problems and the proposals made to solve them into better perspective.

In the United States approximately 75,000 newborn babies die each year. In 1968 our infant death rate of 21.17 per 100,000 live births exceeded that of 14 other countries, some of which maintain a rate of only 12 per 1,000. Nonwhite babies of this country die at a rate nearly double that for white babies. American mothers die in childbirth at a rate exceeding that of 11 other countries. Nonwhite American mothers die in childbirth at a rate four times the rate of white American mothers. American males have a shorter life expectancy than the males of 19 other industrialized countries;

American females have a shorter life expectancy than the females of six other industrialized countries. Nonwhite Americans have a life expectancy seven years shorter than that of white Americans. American males at age 40 are more likely to die before they reach age 50 than males of the same age in 15 other countries. Indeed, the death rate of American males between the ages of 40 and 50 is nearly double that of men of the same age living in Scandinavia. The death rate for nonwhite American males between the ages of 40 and 50 is double that of white American males. These data, and there are many more, have led many observers to conclude that in matters of health we are in fact an underdeveloped nation.

THE FACT THAT WE ARE UNDERDEVELOPED is especially galling because to many of us it appears that we have the potential to achieve a healthy population and to provide excellent health services. And it is even further galling to realize that

The author is Professor of Maternal and Child Health in the School of Public Health at the University of North Carolina at Chapel Hill and until recently was Vice-Chancellor for Health Affairs at UNC-CH. This address was made before the Legislative Orientation Conference in December.

this unhappy record of health services is achieved with a national expenditure rate for health services which exceeds that of nearly every other nation in the world. A record of poor health may be more closely related to matters of poverty than to matters of medical care. But they are not unrelated, and increasingly people of every socioeconomic circumstance freely reveal their frustration with efforts to obtain personal health services of a quality they had been led to expect. There are many communities where the services are incomplete or, what's worse, available only at great inconvenience, loss of dignity, and sometimes shocking personal cost. Although the crisis we describe has received a great deal of public attention in recent years, it dates back for an extended period —at least from World War II.

Immediately after World War II a succession of national efforts was made to improve both the quality of health services and the immediate availability of health care for Americans. Many have benefited in both North Carolina and every other part of the country, but clearly they have been incomplete and inadequate in making substantial reversals in some of the health care trends I have described.

One of the most ambitious programs undertaken immediately after the war was one to build hospitals, with heavy emphasis on construction in rural areas, in small towns—particularly in the South and the Middle West—so that now it seems almost as if there is not a county anywhere that has not a least one 30- or 40-bed hospital built with matching federal funds. These hospitals have had limited value. In many communities they are poorly utilized; occupancy rates are below 20 or 30 per cent, with exorbitant costs for care of the few patients seen there. In fact, because of the small staff and the small size, the services themselves are incomplete and the hospitals have become, if not vacant, little more than nursing homes. The construction of rural hospitals was a major undertaking and I think perhaps a very necessary one, but it has not improved the quality of care nor attracted physicians into rural areas

and small towns to the extent that many people had hoped.

At about the same time new attention was focused on American medical schools. During this period medical education and medical schools were expanding tremendously. Nearly every two-year medical school in the country, including the one at the University of North Carolina, converted to four-year curriculum, with major construction and expansion programs. American medical schools were not then, and are not now, in a healthy state as far as financing is concerned. They tend to be heavily financed from research grants and from the clinical practice of faculty members. They have never been well financed with direct support to medical education. During the years immediately after World War II an enormous amount of money was poured into medical schools, largely to support research efforts. At that time the public bias against federal support for education, even federal support for medical education, was strong, and it seemed that the only way that the National Institutes of Health and the Public Health Services could aid medical schools was to give financial aid indirectly to their research activities rather than direct support to their educational programs. Research has its own abundant justifications, but it is a poor device for supporting medical education. The imbalances that have resulted in many medical schools continue to be a source of concern to many observers.

BOTH THEN AND NOW efforts have been made, again at the federal level, to remove some of the financial barriers toward adequate medical care through a whole host of programs. It is hard to estimate the total share of government spending in the nation's health bill. Before Medicaid and Medicare began, around 35 or 40 per cent of the total medical bill in this country was paid through one governmental mechanism or another. Surely the percentage is much higher now, exceeding probably 50 per cent, through various programs of reimbursement, federal subsidy to state agencies that render health services, and extensive medical care programs in VA hospitals and the armed services. Also, reimbursement for purchase of service through private insurance mechanisms and through Medicaid and Medicare have achieved tremendous prominence. Many observers are disappointed with the results, and I concur. Increasing the consumer's ability to buy services is not a sufficient solution to the problem. If the services themselves are

2

not expanded and made more available to the consumer, he is not much benefited. In fact, one can argue that unless the capacity to render services is increased, such payment mechanisms are inflationary; they increase the cost of care that in the long run is improved neither in quality nor in availability.

The program now being discussed as the grandest one of all for removing financial barriers to medical care is a national compulsory health Insurance. How surprising that an issue which 25 years ago would not have been tolerated in open discussion and would have been quickly labeled a socialized scheme is now so acceptable to such a large segment of the American public. Labor unions, for example, like national compulsory health insurance because it removes the cost of medical care benefits from the bargaining tables. Industry likes it because it transfers the responsibility for the cost of its medical care programs from industry to government. Consumers like it because they believe it will pay their bills. Increasingly physicians and health professionals like it because they see it as a mechanism of reimbursement for patterns of service as they exist today rather than for some more drastic or radical solutions to medical care. Whether all these happy expectations can be fulfilled is problematic. Our record with payment schemes that do not provide services is not a happy one.

IN RECENT YEARS, in addition to these efforts to improve services, a few others, largely initiated at the national level, have been made to improve or increase the degree of planning around medical care in order that our patterns of care might be less haphazard, less duplicative, less prone to large gaps in both kinds of services and their geographic distribution. One of these was the Regional Medical Program, now a half-dozen years old. The aim of this program was to promote, on a regional basis, careful planning of services for both peripheral primary care and sophisticated centralized care to close the gap between what was known to be good medical care and what the people were actually receiving with special reference to three major health problems—heart disease, cancer, and stroke. In the past six years the Regional Medical Programs have achieved a good deal in terms of continuing education, planning, and organization; but I think that one could not claim that this effort has substantially altered the availability of medical care to most Americans.

Disappointments with Regional Medical Care led very quickly to yet another national program, Comprehensive Health Planning. To the observer it appeared almost as if Washington was throwing up its hands in desperation, saying: We cannot improve health care by any of the mechanisms we have tried—building hospital beds, increased reimbursement, regional planning. We will now make funds available and require that planning be done on a state and local basis. So state offices of Comprehensive Health Planning were started. The job they have before them is absolutely monumental, and some real benefits have come about; but again I think that the benefits have not made dramatic changes in the availability of health care to the people in the areas served.

DURING THE SIXTIES increased attention had been paid to health manpower in the hope and belief that somehow by increasing the numbers of doctors, nurses, and physicians' assistants—or possibly by changing their geographic distribution, or by changing their character in other ways, emphasizing general practitioners—improved health services will result. We should pay attention to a background of experience with similar efforts.

The first real alarm that sounded a doctor shortage and urged a dramatic increase in health manpower was the Bane Report, published in 1959. That report provided data on the numbers of doctors in the country and projected the nation's population growth. At that time across the country there were about 130 doctors per 100,000 population. Projecting the population growth through 1975, the report stated that in order to maintain the then-existing ratio of physicians to population it would be necessary to establish twenty-five new medical schools and dramatically expand the enrollment of existing ones. That seemed like an almost impossible undertaking In 1958, but as we approach 1975, it is interesting how closely that goal has been achieved. Many new medical schools have expanded their enrollments far beyond what anyone had thought possible. (We have also continued to attract a substantial number of foreign medical graduates, which has problems all of its own; nevertheless this influx has contributed to the pool of manpower). But most significantly, the growth of the American population was much less during this period than demographers had projected. The result is that between 1959 and 1970 a striking improvement in the ratio of doctors to population has occurred. Instead of the 130:100,000 ratio of 1959, the national ratio, according to AMA statistics not yet published but available on inquiry, is 160 doctors per 100,000 population. This is an increase in the number of doctors far beyond what anybody had thought possible. What the Bane report urged was that we strive to maintain a constant ratio. We did much better—we improved it. But one must ask whether the quality and availability of health services have improved. I think that there is a great deal to suggest that they have not. Nor is there much evidence that health services are improved in areas of greatest concentration of physicians.

During the same time efforts were made both to change the distribution of doctors and to alter the character and content of medical education with a view to manipulating the career choices of young physicians. This has been tried conscientiously in a number of states and in a number of medical schools. One of the first was the University of Kansas, which made an enormous effort to place general practitioners in small towns. Hill-Burton funds and the Sears Roebuck Foundation helped build clinics in every county seat in western Kansas. The medical school brought onto its faculty a number of general practitioners and required every student to spend a period of clinical instruction working with a general practitioner in a town of less than 2,500 population. Faculty members toured the state giving lectures and seminars for practitioner-preceptors to help update their medical knowledge. That program went on for a dozen years and more, and what was its effect? That state has exactly the same problems of locating doctors in small towns as any other. Precisely the same proportion of graduates from that medical school are involved in specialized metropolitan practice as from any other medical school. Those efforts have not been conspicuously successful, and neither have others. In Kansas and in every other place I know only one criterion can be used to predict whether doctors will be attracted to a site for practice: Is it an area of economic growth? As with many kinds of public service—whether they involve lawyers, physicians, educators, or bankers—people are attracted to growing communities and flourishing prospects; they are not attracted to areas of declining population and deteriorating personal and public services.

Besides this emphasis upon increasing the number of physicians, distributed in different ways in relation to both professional interest and location, attention has been given to expanding the scope and quality of their services by surrounding them with assistants (physicians' assistants or nurse practitioners) who can do many things the doctor has done, thereby enabling him to care for larger numbers of people. This is an attractive concept—one that has been tried experimentally, particularly with nurse practitioners in Colorado and with physicians' assistants from Duke University. Nevertheless Dr. Eugene Stead, who has sponsored and guided the physician's assistant program at Duke, said in a recent conference that we must be cautious about how much the physician's assistant or nurse practitioner can solve our problems. These people do not yet exist, or they exist only in such small numbers that we cannot yet say what their full impact will be on the quantity and quality of medical care. With reference to the Duke program, I think there is only one community where a physician's assistant is clearly and conspicuously a success. Most of the other trainees, perhaps 30 in all, are established in hospitals or other situations where assessing their value in expanding medical care is difficult.

The critical factor in medical care is not so much the number of doctors or other professionals as how they deliver their services—whether in a systematic and organized way. I submit that this applies also to the physician's assistant. Is he working in a pattern or a structure of medical care? If he is not, gaps in health care will remain and no amount of manpower will close them. "When a system for health care lacks effectiveness, it means, among other things, that health personnel are not being used effectively. This presents a dilemma to educators who want to develop an educational system relevant to health need. If personnel are educated to meet the need but the health service provides no opportunity to use their competence, what then?" [Bryant, **Health and the Developing World** (Ithaca: Cornell University Press, 1969).]

THIS MATTER OF SYSTEMS OF CARE, which is beginning to attract wide attention, is very important to future efforts to improve the quality of medical care. But in moving to this discussion I want not to leave the impression that increasing the number of doctors and other kinds of manpower is not urgently necessary. What I am saying is that expansion by itself holds very little promise for solving our problems. What may hold promise is placing these increased numbers of graduates in some kind of pattern of care different from what we have now.

Let me tell you something about the patterns of care that seem to present most successes. There is a 25-year experience now with prepaid group practices, started on the West Coast by the Kaiser Industries. Unlike an insurance plan which pays the bills for a patient, provided he can go out and find the services somewhere, the prepaid group practice scheme collects premiums from the patients and delivers the services directly. This is done by a group of physicians and other health personnel, usually clustered around a hospital. The plan is committed to providing total medical care to a defined population group. Experience suggests that this system is far more economical than the more random patterns of care ordinarily available in this country and that it emphasizes preventive medicine much more than random care does. It seems to eliminate some unnecessary kinds of medical attention, and it has produced improved levels of service according to most ways that we have for measuring it. Probably most observers would agree that this is an important pattern of service for some people in some situations but no one would claim that it is broadly satisfactory, to be provided widely across the country in an indiscriminant and uniform way.

A second new pattern of care started first in metropolitan ghetto areas as the comprehensive neighborhood health center. Efforts are being made, most notably by the University of North Carolina, to apply this same concept to small town and rural areas. Again for a defined population group and a defined geographic area a clinic is established and staffed, all with its own personnel (physicians, home health visitors, and home health aides, etc.). A crucial aspect of the program is the training of people from the defined community as health aides. They help guide their neighbors into the health-delivery system and assist their understanding and interpretation of the care. The comprehensive neighborhood health center has proved to be an impressive and desirable pattern of care for some people in some situations.

Other patterns of care have had effectiveness and probably should be more widely applied in states like ours. Many groups of physicians in county medical societies organize and establish themselves into a foundation or a corporation which assumes responsibility for total medical care.

And finally, some of us believe that for some parts of our country, some communities, some rural areas, it is difficult to conceive any pattern of care that can meet the needs of the people short of direct provision of services through some unit of government, very likely through the expanded services of a district or county health department. I invite your attention, as a matter of fact, to the services of health departments in North Carolina. They exercise a surprising degree of local autonomy compared with such units in other states. That is obviously desirable from many points of view, but it is undesirable from others in that enormous gaps in services occur. Some local health departments provide superb services; their neighboring health department may provide virtually none at all. Some mechanism for uniformly improving the services would seem worthwhile. Some kinds of service, such as home health care, are not easily provided through any other mechanism than public health departments.

A FURTHER, CRITICAL POINT: We must be careful not to expect too much of medical services. Are we trying to solve problems with medical care that ought in fact to be solved with improved housing, improved nutrition, improved recreation, and improved education. Disease and bad health are results of deficiencies in any of these categories; efforts to correct deficiencies of poverty by means of expensive medical care can hardly be successful.

ASIDE FROM GENERAL CONCERNS about the quality of life, there are indeed immediate concerns about medical care. In my view, improvements will not come about except through the organization of medical care and the incorporation of every citizen into some organized system of care. Ideally these systems will be locally designed and controlled, each according to local needs and precedents. We already know some systems that could be more extensively applied; we need to develop others. I make no brief for a uniform national plan that can be expected to serve the various local needs for this diversified country. But neither do I hold hope for medical care based entirely on random career choices of individual professionals.

Development of a network of local systems of care will be a long and arduous task. In the meantime, some specifics can be accomplished. Are school health services all that they should be in North Carolina? Other countries have found comprehensive school health services to be efficient mechanisms for the prevention and early identification of disorders. But school health services in a given town may consist of little more than a

(Continued on Page 25)

REMOVAL OF JUDGES

REPORT

of the

COURTS COMMISSION

to the

1971 GENERAL ASSEMBLY

part 2

In North Carolina appellate and superior court judges may be removed from office by impeachment or, if the cause be mental or physical incapacity, by "joint resolution of two-thirds of all the members of each house of the General Assembly."[1] District court judges cannot be impeached, but may be removed for misconduct or mental or physical incapacity as provided by law. The law (G.S. 7A-143) provides for a due process hearing before a superior court judge with right of appeal. There is no formal means for disciplining any judge, short of removal, and impeachment is the sole means for removing an appellate or superior court judge for misconduct.

Impeachment is not only ill suited for its purpose but also ineffective. No judge has been removed by the impeachment route in this state since 1862.[2] The procedure is cumbersome, equivalent to a grand jury of 120 and a petty jury of 50, with the latter empowered to overrule the judge by majority vote. It is expensive. (In Florida, two fairly recent impeachment trials — both unsuccessful — cost over a quarter of a million dollars.) Impeachment is appropriate for only the most severe misconduct and, perhaps for this reason, frequently fails. Finally, it is in reality a political rather than a judicial device, and frequently tainted with partisanship.

The "joint resolution" procedure, while limited to disability cases, is even less effective. Apparently it has never been used in North Carolina, and its use is so unlikely that it lacks even a deterrent effect.

---

1. The "joint resolution" procedure is nowadays quite generally referred to as "address," although the latter term originally referred to a joint resolution addressed to the executive who was supposed to effect the removal. Many state constitutions have dropped the feature of executive participation.

2. Chief Justice Furches and Associate Justice Douglas were impeached in 1901, but the Senate vote for conviction fell short of the two-thirds necessary for conviction. [Clark, *History of the Supreme Court in North Carolina*, 177 N.C. 617, 631.] The House preferred articles of impeachment against Superior Court Judge E. W. Jones in 1871, but later withdrew them. [Hamilton, *Reconstruction in North Carolina*, 561-62 (1964 reprint).] No search has been made earlier than 1868, but before that time judges were selected by joint vote of the members of the General Assembly, and it is reasonable to assume that judges selected by the General Assembly are less likely to be impeached by it than judges elected by the people.

Once we have named a man as a judge, the quality of his performance as a judge passes almost completely outside our effective surveillance and control, unless his performance is extremely bad. . . . Any notion that the public or the bar may have any genuine control over the quality of judicial performance by judges already on the bench is simply not realistic.

Robert A. Leflar, *The Quality of Judges,*
35 IND. L. J. 289, 305 (1960).

Important as it is that people should get justice, it is even more important that they be made to feel and see that they are getting it.

Lord Herschell

. . . no man is as essential to his country's well-being as is the unstained dignity of the courts.

Charles Evan Hughes, Chief Justice
of the United States Supreme Court

. . . the means provided by the system or organic law in America for removing a judge, who for any reason is found to be unfit for his office, is very unsatisfactory. . . . It is very certain that after the experience of nearly a century the remedy by impeachment in the case of judges, perhaps in all cases, must be pronounced utterly inadequate. There are many matters which ought to be causes for removal that are neither treason, bribery, nor high crimes and misdemeanors. Physical infirmities for which a man is not to blame, but which may wholly unfit him for judicial duty, are of the first class. Deafness, loss of sight, the decay of the faculties by reason of age, insanity, prostration by disease from which there is no hope of recovery—these should all be reasons for removal, rather than that the administration of justice should be obstructed or indefinitely suspended.

Justice Samuel Miller (USSC, 1878)

. . . An arbitrary or disagreeable course of action by a judge arises principally from the fact that he is subject to no authority which can receive complaints against him and act upon those complaints by way of private or public criticism and correction of the judge. The best against arbitrary and disagreeable actions by judges is a duly constituted body of fellow judges who hold a position of superior power and authority and to whom complaints as to conduct of judges may be brought and who may investigate those complaints and exercise a corrective influence.

Albert Kales, 52 ANNALS OF THE AMERICAN
ACADEMY OF POLITICAL AND SOCIAL SCIENCE
(1914)

North Carolina has been blessed with a singularly scandal-free judiciary. Other states have been less fortunate. Scandals of major proportions in recent years have afflicted the bench in California, Florida, Illinois, Iowa, Louisiana, Missouri, Michigan, New York, Oklahoma, and other states.[3] Probably part of North Carolina's good fortune has gone unrecognized as pure luck. That fact being so, the question may legitimately be asked—how long will our favorable experience continue? Just a few years ago we had only 45 full-time state-paid judges. We now have 177.[4] To most observers, the need for an efficient

3. But no judge selected by the merit plan in any of these states has been the subject of removal proceedings.

4. This is not necessarily an increase in over-all members; there were many locally paid judges prior to the coming of the district court system.

means of disciplining or removing judges who cannot measure up to the required moral, professional, or physical standards is obvious.

The need for a truly effective mechanism for disciplining or removing judges for misconduct or disability has received increasing attention in recent years. The problem is a very sensitive one, especially to some judges, who are understandably wary that efforts to impose accountability for judicial conduct may interfere with the tradition of independence. Other judges, however, have recognized the larger public interest in the efficient and untainted administration of justice, and realized that in the long run the public's interest and their own are one and the same. The inadequacy of present methods of dealing with judicial misconduct leaves all questions of fitness and conduct to the conscience of the judge or the judgment—frequently uninformed—of the electorate. This unfortunately means that many problems of judicial fitness go unsolved. The erring tendencies of the 1 per cent tarnish the dedication of the 99 per cent, and public esteem in the judiciary is diminished. Both the public and the judiciary suffer from lack of working machinery for discipline or removal of the small minority.

At the outset we would like to make it clear that we are not referring simply to misconduct so gross as to clearly warrant removal. Such misconduct is exceptionally rare, although disproportionately publicized, and by itself does not merit the concern that many states have recently given to the over-all problem of which it is a small part. We are also referring to a kind of judicial misbehavior for which removal is too severe, a kind that can usually be corrected by action within the judicial system without sacrificing the judge. A flexible machinery that can handle minor cases as well as major ones is an urgent and widely felt need. It is considered by some knowledgeable observers to be the most pressing problem facing the twentieth-century judiciary. Such a procedure would be analogous to the censure and disbarment machinery of the organized bar—machinery long ago recognized as essential to protect the image of the legal profession. The sort of conduct we are referring to has been reported in these examples from other states: chronic absenteeism; intemperance; abuse of litigants, witnesses, or defendants; erratic and unseemly courtroom behavior; questionable extrajudicial activities; persistent tardiness; and prolonged and excessive delays in rendering decisions. If these should occur in North Carolina, it is essential for the public good—and the good of the judiciary—that there be some means to deal with them.

We are also referring to another kind of judicial performance—not misconduct, but a blameless kind occasioned by waning of physical and mental powers. This is less common in states with mandatory retirement ages than elsewhere, but it exists in all states.

It is almost invariably unrecognized by its victims, most of whom have served long and honorably and who are entitled to a liberal retirement allowance. A mandatory retirement age will lessen this problem, but not eliminate it. Shrinking physical vigor and mental acuity occur at different ages in different men, and an outstanding judge of diminishing vigor and long years may still be better than a young and vigorous judge of meager talents. The point remains that, at whatever age, infirmity overtakes all men, and an objective means is needed to assess those cases in which physical or mental decline prevents effective performance. In these cases, the customary solution, upon prompting, is voluntary retirement. In those rare instances in which voluntary retirement is resisted, there should be power to force retirement. Of course, entitlement to retirement compensation would be protected.

Judicial Qualifications Commission

Machinery to discipline, remove, or retire the unfit or disabled judge, in addition to or in lieu of impeachment and address, has been established in at least twenty-five states in the past quarter-century. The most successful system has been set up by California. It has been so widely copied that it deserves special mention.

In California, a constitutional amendment of 1960 authorized a judicial qualifications commission. The qualifications commission consists of five trial and appellate judges, two attorneys, and two public (non-lawyer) members. It is authorized to receive complaints concerning the conduct or performance of any judge in the state, and it may initiate investigation of alleged misconduct or disability on its own motion. It answers all complaints. About 90 per cent of them involve a litigant disgruntled over a judge's decision in a particular case; these the commission terminates with an explanatory letter.[5] In the small minority of complaints an investigation is conducted. If minor misconduct is verified it is almost always corrected by informal correspondence or an interview with the judge concerned. If major misconduct, or physical or mental disability is suspected, a formal, due process hearing may be offered the judge. At this stage, if not earlier, the judge usually resigns or retires. The commission is authorized to recommend formal censure, removal, or retirement to the Supreme Court of California. Until such recommendations are made, all proceedings are confidential.

In the first four years of the commission's existence, 26 judges retired while under investigation; in the first seven years, 44 judges; in the first nine years, 50 judges.[6] During this period, only one judge was

---

5. The commission has no jurisdiction over a judge's decision in a particular case (unless bribery or outright fraud is alleged), that being a matter for appeal.
6. California has over 1,600 judges, or about six times as many as North Carolina. Equivalent figures for North Carolina would average no more than one judge per year.

recommended for removal, and the state supreme court rejected the recommendation. Formal censure as a means of handling misconduct not severe enough to warrant dismissal was added to the commission's powers in 1966 and has been employed successfully in two cases since then. Most of the resignations or retirements occasioned by the qualifications commission's operations so far have been due to mental or physical disability, including intemperance. Few have been due to specific acts of misconduct.

Leadership for adoption of the qualifications commission plan in California was furnished by Chief Justice Phil Gibson. The plan was also supported by a 364 to 34 vote of the California Conference of Judges and adopted by a 3 to 1 vote of the people. In campaigning for the proposal, Justice Gibson said: "No honest and industrious judge who has the mental and physical capacity to perform his duties has anything to fear" from the commission method of removal. "Surely the people have the right to expect that every judge will be honest and industrious and that no judge will be permitted to remain on the bench if he suffers from physical or mental infirmity which seriously interferes with the performance of his judicial duties."

The key to the success of the qualifications commission plan lies in the operations of the qualifications commission. For complaints that appear to have some merit, the procedure has been described as follows:

Under the California practice the letter procedure is a part of the investigatory function but it is only undertaken after careful consideration and when there is an apparently credible dereliction or condition of some significance calling for explanation.

The judge's reply may be completely satisfactory, in which case the confidential file will so show and be closed, or the reply or perhaps failure to reply may show the necessity for further investigation and may ultimately lead to removal proceedings.

Another possibility is that the allegations while valid are not grave enough to justify taking further action and there may be reason to think that there will be an improvement. Sometimes there may be reason to accept the plea, "I didn't do it, but I'll see it doesn't happen again."

Depending upon circumstances, the closing of the matter can be conditioned upon the cessation of the impropriety. If the situation warrants, and only occasionally should this be necessary, the matter can be held and then rechecked before closing.

None of this is foolproof but it does provide an avenue so that discipline in a very positive way can be a factor in the improvement of the judicial machinery. To what extent a commis-

sion chooses to function in that sphere rests in the sound discretion of its members.[7]

Another factor in the success and acceptance of the California plan is the confidentiality of the proceedings. This is provided for in the state's constitution. Information concerning a case cannot be made public until after a due process hearing and a recommendation for censure or removal is filed with the supreme court. This is essential to protect the good judge against unjustified public attack, and it lets the disabled or unethical judge retire or resign without public disgrace that would cast unfair reflection on the bench in general. It also aids investigations by assuring potential complainants that they need not fear repercussions. Experience in California has shown that unless the judge under investigation himself chooses to make the matter public, there are no leaks. Nearly all of the states with plans similar to California's have included this confidentiality feature.

Provisions for the discipline, retirement, or removal of judges, in addition to or in substitution for traditional methods, now exist in over half of the states. The plan adopted by most jurisdictions follows that of California. These states are Alaska, Colorado, Florida, Idaho, Illinois, Louisiana, Maryland, Michigan, Nebraska, New Mexico, Ohio, Oregon, Pennsylvania, Texas, Utah, and Vermont.[8] To this list Arizona, Indiana, Missouri, and Virginia can be added as a result of November, 1970, elections. Puerto Rico also has such a plan, and Congress prescribed a Commission on Judicial Disabilities and Tenure for the courts of the District of Columbia in 1970. The plan is under active consideration in several more states.

The chief virtues of the judicial qualifications commission plan seem to be these:

(1) The commission offers a flexible, fair, efficient and inexpensive means of dealing with physical and mental infirmities, and with misconduct, whether it be aggravated or minor. The provisions for confidentiality and three of his own kind on the commission assure each judge of fairness and freedom from harrassment.

(2) The existence of the commission with its power to recommend censure, retirement, or removal acts as a powerful deterrent to the occasional judge who might otherwise fall short of the standards expected. An easily accessible procedure for airing complaints and taking corrective action can have a salutary effect that the distant and unreal threat of impeachment never had.

7. Frankel, The Case for Judicial Disciplinary Measures, 49 A.B.A.J. 218, 219 (1966).
8. A few states, typified by New York, Delaware and Oklahoma, have a court on the judiciary. The court on the judiciary works on an ad hoc basis, processes only the most serious matters, and is more formal and cumbersome. A few states also have special procedures for processing disability cases only. Information about each state's procedures is collected in the American Judicature Society's Report No. 5, JUDICIAL DISCIPLINE AND REMOVAL (August, 1969). This report also contains an excellent bibliography.

(3) The commission provides a safety valve for disgruntled litigants and others who might otherwise cause serious loss of confidence in the courts. They can ventilate their grievances without unfairly harming a particular judge. A sympathetic letter of explanation from an official public agency serves to soften or dissipate the ire of many complainants.

(4) The public is assured of an honest, able, efficient bench, yet the independence of the judiciary is fully protected. And since the system permits the judiciary to police its own ranks, with any decision to censure, remove, or retire coming from the supreme court, the temptation of the executive or legislative branches to involve themselves in these matters is minimized.

A Judicial Standards[9] Commission For North Carolina

Adoption of a workable method for censuring and removing unworthy or disabled judges in North Carolina requires a constitutional amendment. However, the traditional methods of impeachment and address for removing judges need not be done away with—they can remain in the Constitution for assurance to the people of their ultimate power, acting through their elected representatives. It is necessary only to add a provision authorizing an additional procedure for discipline and removal of judges for misconduct or disability. The Commission recommends insertion of the following language in Article IV, section 17:

(2) *Additional method of removal of Judges.* The General Assembly shall prescribe a procedure, in addition to impeachment and address set forth in this section, for the removal of a Justice or Judge of the General Court of Justice for mental or physical incapacity interfering with the performance of his duties which is, or is likely to become, permanent, and for the censure and removal of a Justice or Judge of the General Court of Justice for wilful misconduct in office, wilful and persistent failure to perform his duties, habitual intemperance, conviction of a crime involving moral turpitude, or conduct prejudicial to the administration of justice that brings the judicial office into disrepute.

The Courts Commission feels that the grounds for censure or removal of a judge are so fundamental that they should be imbedded in the Constitution. Other matters, such as the creation and composition of a Judicial Standards Commission and its procedures, are better left to the wisdom of the General Assembly. This general arrangement has been followed by most of the states with bodies of this type.

9. We prefer the name Judicial Standards Commission to Judicial Qualifications Commission.

The Courts Commission recommends that a Judicial Standards Commission be created by statute, and that it be composed of representatives of bench, bar, and the general public. The General Court of Justice should be represented by one judge from each of its divisions—appellate, superior court, and district court. The appellate division judge should come from the Court of Appeals. (This does not overlook the Supreme Court; it participates in the removal process when it receives and reviews the recommendations of the Standards Commission.) Each of these judge-members should be appointed by the Chief Justice of the Supreme Court. The bar would be represented by two attorneys who have practiced in the courts of the state for at least ten years, and who presumably thereby have acquired the experience and judgment vital to a proper discharge of their sensitive roles. They would be elected by the State Bar Council, the governing body of the integrated bar of the state, whose 30 members are themselves elected by the lawyers of the various judicial districts. To give the Commission balance and objectivity, two public members would be appointed by the Governor. The chairman of this seven-man commission would be the Court of Appeals judge.

To assure continuity of commission membership, members would serve overlapping terms of six years. No full-term member could succeed himself. Vacancies would be filled in the same manner as the original appointment. Members would serve without compensation other than the per diem and expenses afforded members of state boards and commissions generally.

The grounds for censure or removal of a justice or judge are those basic violations set forth in a majority of the state statutes establishing removal bodies: willful misconduct in office, willful and persistent failure to perform the duties of the office, habitual intemperance, and conduct prejudicial to the administration of justice that brings the judicial office into disrepute. The latter category is designed to cover willful and persistent violations of the canons of professional ethics applicable to the judiciary, transgressions which are not necessarily covered by the earlier categories. To these grounds has been added "conviction of a crime involving moral turpitude," out of an abundance of caution and because it is arguable that such misconduct is not altogether covered by "willful misconduct in office." A judge could also be removed for mental or physical disability of a permanent, or likely to be permanent, nature. A judge removed for mental or physical reasons, however, would be entitled to retirement compensation if he was qualified for it under any provisions of state law; a judge removed for misconduct would not be so entitled, although a judge facing formal removal proceedings would have the

(Continued on Page 21)

JAILS IN NORTH CAROLINA

BY CLIFTON M. CRAIG

This article by the North Carolina Commissioner of Social Services is reprinted from **Social Services** for December, 1970.

The terms "jail" and "prison" have become synonymous to many people in North Carolina. This is easy to see when one reads a newspaper article about confinement facilities. The writer will in one sentence use the term "jail" and in another making reference to the same facility use the word "prison." Do the two terms properly refer to the same facility?

At one time, jails were institutions used to detain suspected or arrested offenders until they could be tried by the courts. However, another type of facility called the "house of correction" and used primarily as a place of punishment for minor offenders evolved in England during the fifteenth and sixteenth centuries. During the eighteenth century in England the jail and the "house of correction" gradually merged and often were located under the same roof and administered by the same person. The jail thus became not only a place for the temporary detention of suspects but also a prison for convicted petty offenders and vagrants.

What was, and still exists in some places

The early settlers of America brought with them the customs and institutions of their mother countries. For example, the treatment of offenders included sentences to jail, the whipping post, the pillory, the stocks, and the ducking stool. Imprisonment, as such, was of short duration and limited to the lesser offenders.

In Colonial America and North Carolina practically all serious crimes were punished by death or some form of corporal punishment. Penal administration in North Carolina did not require an elaborate organization or highly trained personnel. Every county was required by law to build "a courthouse, prison, and stocks." The sheriff apprehended offenders, the county court and local justices of the peace tried them and imposed sentence, and the sheriff carried it out.

The first real turning point in North Carolina's confinement program came about in 1868. Apart from directing the General Assembly to make provisions for a state prison, the Constitution in that year abolished corporal punishment in all forms and limited the death penalty to four crimes (arson, murder, rape, and burglary).

As corporal punishment gave way to imprisonment, it became apparent that a separate prison system would be established by the state. Thus, the administration of prison punishment, borne almost entirely by the counties prior to 1868 with some help from cities and towns, began to shift to the state. The shift continued as the state prison system expanded, with separate plants and buildings for separate classes of offenders from 1907 through the present.

Local jails shifted back to a facility for detention of those awaiting trial and those found guilty of misdemeanor. Prisons became the place for confinement of criminals and those found guilty of more serious crimes.

So, as we look at the two terms today, we see that they are not synonymous because they serve two completely separate governments. The state operates prisons and the counties and cities operate jails.

Thus, in considering jails in North Carolina we are talking about places where almost any citizen could find himself temporarily while trying to make bond after an accident or trying to reach relatives or a lawyer after even a minor incident resulting in a charge requiring a later court appearance.

During the period following the Constitution of 1868, North Carolina began developing a separate prison system. But at the same time this system was improving, the local jails were deteriorating.

The Board of Public Charities (later named Board of Public Welfare) was given the responsibility for the inspection of these jails, but was never given any authority to do anything about their condition until 1967. That year, the North Carolina General Assembly adopted its historic local jail legislation. It gave the Department of Public Welfare, now the Department of Social Services, the responsibility for developing and enforcing minimum jail standards and developing training for personnel operating these jails. It made it compulsory that local jails abide by these standards and also have their personnel participate in the training program. The Commissioner of the Department was given the authoritiy to close jails that did not meet the new standards.

The same 1967 session of the General Assembly created a Jail Study Commission to make recommendations to the 1969 session as to further improvement they found necessary in local jails in North Carolina.

This Commission issued its report to the 1969 session which included twenty recommendations for the further improvement of local confinement facilities in North Carolina.

Fifteen separate bills were introduced, one of them calling for the removal of the Jail and Detention Services from the then Department of Public Welfare.

The Commission gave two reasons for this recommendation. First, it stated, "Jail inspectors find that their advice is often unwanted and unheeded by local officials because the service is tied, in the public's mind, with unrelated and less popular programs of the Department of Public Welfare. If the service were put elsewhere, then this factor at least would not diminish in advance the influence of its personnel in obtaining improvements in local jails." Second, the report stated, "We believe that the jail inspection program could, in exposing inadequate jail conditions, arouse controversy on the local level that might upset the Department's relations with local officials whose cooperation is essential for the Department's important program in public assistance and child welfare. If the Department continues to contain the jail and detention service, it could be faced in the future with a situation where it would wish to avoid taking disruptive action in the enforcement of jail standards in order to retain local support for its other programs. In this manner, jail improvements in some places could be delayed for many years and thereby thwart the General Assembly's intent, as shown by the authorization of minimum jail

standards in 1967 to have all local detention facilities meet those standards as rapidly as possible.

WHAT HAS HAPPENED?

The Joint Senate and House Committee on Correctional Institutions gave an unfavorable report to the bill that would have removed the jail and detention service from the Department of Social Services and placed it in another State department. It also gave unfavorable reports to nine of the other bills submitted on jail improvement.

Have the two reasons the Study Commission gave for removing the Jail and Detention Service from the Department of Social Services proved valid? Have jail improvements been delayed for many years and the General Assembly's intent been thwarted by the jail and detention service remaining in the Department of Social Services? Has the jail legislation passed by the 1967 General Assembly caused progress to be made in local confinement facilities throughout the State?

Let us examine the actual facts.

Since the jail legislation passed by the 1967 General Assembly became law, many significant changes have taken place.

When the 1967 session was held, there was only one jail inspector on the Department staff. The session appropriated funds for a staff of ten members including a chief of the section, a training officer, a technical assistant, an administrative assistant, four district inspectors and two clerical workers.

At present there are 95 county jails, 100 municipal jails, and seven juvenile detention centers that are inspected at least twice a year by the jail and detention services section.

In addition to their inspection function, section staff members serve as consultants to counties and cities in the area of jail construction and renovation, and conduct training programs for jail personnel in

compliance with the required training program established by the General Assembly.

Reports indicate that during the fiscal year 1969-70 255,000 persons were confined in the local jails of this state. Of this total number there were 1,207 juveniles under sixteen years of age, 1,833 mental cases, and 35 deaths including 11 suicides.

The new jail standards called for by the 1967 General Assembly were completed and approved by former Governor Dan Moore on November 6, 1968. This culminated months of work by a committee that helped the staff develop the standards. Representatives of the N. C. Association of County Commissioners, N. C. League of Municipalities, N. C. Sheriffs' Association, N. C. Police Executives Association, N. C. Department of Corrections, State Board of Health, the Insurance Department and Community Colleges served on this committee.

Copies of these standards were sent to all concerned local officials, and the new jail and detention improvement program in North Carolina began to bring immediate action by the beginning of 1969.

JAIL CONSTRUCTION AND RENOVATION

Statistics on new jail construction alone indicate the outstanding cooperation on the part of local governments that has taken place in just a short period of time.

From 1941 through 1968 there were only 28 new county jails constructed in this state. This was an average of only one new jail per year. But during the two years 1969 and 1970 eight counties constructed and opened new jails at a cost of approximately $6 million. In addition three new municipal jails were built. There are presently eight county jails and one juvenile detention center under construction at a cost of $2.5 million. Sixteen counties have already hired architects and are completing plans

The new Cabarrus County jail

for building new jails at a total cost
of $8 million.

This means that while only 28
new county jails were built over
a 28-year period through 1968,
32 new county jails have either
been built or are under construction or architects have been hired
and plans being finalized, all within a two year period.

During this year seven counties
whose jails failed to meet the
standards are in the process of re-
novating their jails in order to
make them acceptable, and one
county has completed renovation.
Six other counties renovated their
jails in 1969.

In February of 1970, 22 counties
were classified as needing new jails
and no action taken by local
officials. At present only 12 counties remain in this category. In
February of 1970, 31 county jails
needed renovation with no action
taken; this number has decreased
to 24 at present.

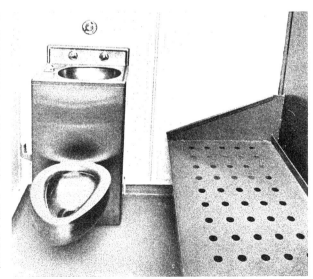

14

COUNTY JAIL IMPROVEMENT, 1969-70

New Jails Opened

Gaston	Mecklenburg	Granville	Rowan
Hoke	Wake	Alexander	Cabarrus

New Jails Under Construction

Davie	Stanly	Union	Onslow
Beaufort	Macon	Wilkes	Iredell

Have Architects Employed

Brunswick	Caswell	Columbus	Transylvania
Camden	Cherokee	Cumberland	Watauga
Pasquotank	Clay	Rutherford	Avery
Perquimans	Cleveland	Stokes	Ashe

Renovation Completed

Montgomery	Orange	Forsyth	Halifax
Moore	Person	Iredell	

Renovation in Process

Alamance	Gates	Greene	Wilson
Anson	Chowan	Vance	

Commissioner Clifton M. Craig has closed four county jails since the new standards went into effect. These were Burke, Columbus, Avery and Davie. Since those jails were closed, Davie has begun construction, Avery and Columbus have hired architects, and Burke has still taken no action.

Plans for North Carolina's first regional jail have been finalized, and Camden, Perquimans and Pasquotank counties plan to start construction of the Albemarle Regional Jail by March 1, 1971. It will be located at Elizabeth City and will cost approximately $450,000. The three counties will be aided by grants of $173,236 from the Governor's Law and Order Committee and $23,240 from the Department of Social Services.

The money for the grant from the Department of Social Services was part of the $200,000 appropriated by the 1969 General Assembly to aid local government in jail improvement. Twenty-eight other local governments shared the remainder of the funds, which they matched two for one to upgrade their jails and juvenile detention centers. The Department of Social Services is requesting $700,000 for this purpose from the 1971 General Assembly to further aid local governments in upgrading their jails.

JAIL PERSONNEL TRAINING

G.S. 153-53.5, enacted by the 1967 General Assembly, states in part: "No person shall serve as jailer or supervise or administer a local confinement facility unless he has successfully completed an approved course of training . . . except on a temporary or probationary basis. No person shall serve on a temporary or probationary basis for more than one year."

Since the inception of the training program in 1968, over 1,600 persons have attended at least one of the varied training sessions held throughout the state. Commissioner Craig has issued 1,450 certificates to jail and detention related employees indicating that they have completed a course of training in compliance with the statute.

Courses in varied aspects of jail management have been made available by the Department of Social Services working in close cooperation with the North Carolina Department of Community Colleges. The Law Enforcement Training Division of the Department of Community Colleges has worked closely with the Social Services Department in providing classrooms, instructors, and other resources.

Forty-five jail training sessions have been held since February 1968. Attendance has included county commissioners, sheriffs, chiefs of police, law enforcement training students, and employees of sheriff and police departments throughout North Carolina.

In addition to the above training, four juvenile detention workshops have been held along with a statewide conference on juvenile detention.

By using funds allocated in a grant from the Omnibus Crime Control and Safe Streets Act in the sum of $69,150, the Department of Social Services plans to sponsor specialized training for sheriffs, chiefs of police, and head jailers in 1971. This will be in addition to the present training that will be continued.

THE FUTURE CHALLENGE

The statistics provided in this article show the great strides that are being taken to improve local confinement facilities in North Carolina. We feel that with the legislation enacted by the 1967 General Assembly and the funds appropriated by the 1969 General Assembly to aid local governments in jail improvement, we now have one of the most progressive jail improvement programs in the country.

Even with these great strides during the past two years, we still cannot rest on our laurels. Twelve counties need new jails and 24 others need either minor or major renovation to be acceptable. We still have very inadequate juvenile detention facilities, as evidenced by over 1,200 juveniles who were

(Continued on Page 25)

summary:

Report and Recommendations of the Commission for the Study of the Local and Ad Valorem Tax Structure of the State of North Carolina

Report

Although many different points of view were expressed by those who appeared before the Commission and by members of the Commission, agreement seemed fairly general on certain frequently mentioned subjects. Among those most often heard were the following:

1. The Machinery Act needs to be recodified—primarily for clarification and logical arrangement, but also to revise obsolete provisions so as to bring them into line with modern practices. (The Commission concluded that although the present act is basically sound in most of its essential provisions, the lack of clarity of some of its parts and deficiencies in others give rise to unequal treatment of taxpayers, often varying between taxing jurisdictions. See Recommendation III, below.)

2. The portions of the Machinery Act concerned with the appraisal of railroads and public service companies need to be modernized, and provision should be made for the central appraisal of the rolling stock of bus lines and motor freight carriers and the flight equipment of air carriers. (Two earlier commissions had recommended improvement in this area, and this Commission concurred that changes are urgently needed. The present provisions of the law are out of line with current business practices and accepted appraisal principles. See Recommendation III, below.)

3. There is a decided need for better-trained assessors and greater recognition by governing officials of the importance of appointing and employing qualified tax assessors. (The Commission was encouraged by the efforts that both individual assessors and the North Carolina Association of Assessing Officers are making to improve the quality of their work. But substantial statewide improvement will not be attained until counties recognize the importance of properly trained appraisal personnel. A well-staffed and adequately funded tax office will be essential in the future, and any investment in such a program will pay well. See Recommendation I, below.)

4. More training opportunities for tax assessors and their assistants should be provided, and also standards for qualifying for assessors' positions. (Noting the voluntary work of the Institute of Government and the North Carolina Association of Assessing Officers, the Commission pointed out that opportunities for training should be greatly expanded, should be required of all assessors, and should be coordinated and funded through the State Board of Assessment. See Recommendations I and III, below.)

5. An alternative method for collecting property taxes on motor vehicles is needed. (In lieu of a property tax, the Commission considered the feasibility of an additional license tax to be collected by the Department of Motor Vehicles, and it also considered the imposition of a license tax by counties and cities. A number of problems surround both of these procedures, and the Commission could not resolve them in the time avail-

16

POPULAR GOVERNMENT

able. See Recommendation II, below.)

6. The 1971 General Assembly should repeal the exemption from ad valorem taxation now accorded the tangible personal property of banks. (The Commission did not deal directly with exemption matters because that subject had been assigned by other 1969 legislation to the Tax Study Commission, but it felt that this policy statement should be made.)

The Commission's chief regret is that within the time allotted, it could not fully explore all of these and many other serious problems involved in the administration of the property tax. It does believe, however, that the proposed recodification of the Machinery Act, which is a part of this report, can be a significant first step in the difficult and complicated task of developing a property tax program administered by trained professionals and respected by all.

Recommendations

- The Commission made three specific recommendations in the following language:

I. The governing bodies of the several local taxing units of this State, exercising the legal authority they now have, should place stronger emphasis on the training, staffing, and compensation of their respective tax departments in order that all property owners may be treated equitably and that the revenues available to local governments from the property tax may be fully realized.

   An expanded training program for tax personnel should be coordinated through the State Board of Assessment, and provision should be made to fund the program adequately.

II. The 1971 General Assembly should provide for continuing the work begun by this Commission by enacting legislation creating a successor commission to function in the 1971-73 biennium and report to the Governor and the 1973 General Assembly.

III. That . . . the Bill Embodying the Commission's Recommendations and Recodification of the Machinery Act be enacted by the 1971 session of the General Assembly.

Expressing the belief that its proposed recodification of the Machinery Act contained a number of significant improvements, the Commission noted that the proposed legislation, among other objectives, was designed to:

1. Provide a clearer and more logical presentation of the duties and responsibilities of tax officials and the duties and rights of taxpayers.

2. Completely revise the statutes providing for railroad and public service company appraisal to (a) bring the law into accord with accepted appraisal principles, (b) provide for the allocation of the property values of such companies on the basis of current business practices, and (c) provide for State Board of Assessment appraisal of products pipeline companies and cable television companies and of the rolling stock of motor carriers and the flight equipment of air carriers.

3. Require that future county tax supervisors be certified by the State Board of Assessment as qualified to perform the duties of the office.

4. Clarify the provision for fourth-year horizontal revaluation of real property.

5. Clarify the statute dealing with discovered property.

6. Authorize the State Board of Assessment to develop and recommend guides and standards for appraising selected categories of property found throughout the State.

7. Provide a means for prompt appeals to the State Board of Assessment from orders of boards of county commissioners adopting schedules of values for use in real property revaluations.

8. Authorize the State Board of Assessment to use hearing officers in handling appeals from valuation and listing decisions of county boards.

9. Revise the tax abstract to permit the use of an affirmation comparable to that used on the income tax return in lieu of the administered oath heretofore required.

10. Strictly regulate the use of agents in listing property for taxation.

11. Advance the tax due date from the first Monday in October to the first day of September.

12. Increase the interest for failure to pay taxes on time from 1 per cent for the first month plus ½ per cent per month thereafter to 2 per cent for the first month and 1 per cent per month thereafter.

13. Revise the garnishment procedure for county and municipal tax collection to bring it into line with the garnishment procedure authorized for the Department of Revenue.

By **Brenda Kinney,**
a recent graduate of Duke University Law School and a research associate at the Institute of Government.

LIABILITY FOR BLOOD TRANSFUSIONS IN NORTH CAROLINA

Currently North Carolina has no laws that deal specifically with an increasingly important area of medical practice and potential professional liability—the collection, storage, and distribution of human blood and the administration of blood transfusions. Recent court decisions in other states suggest that North Carolina should consider clarifying the liability of doctors, hospitals, and blood banks for injuries incurred by patients as a result of transfusions. This article discusses the legal implications of this matter, including some proposed legislative solutions.

Medical advances of recent years have produced an increase in the number of blood transfusions administered to patients, and created an ever growing demand for blood both in North Carolina and throughout the United States. Because it cannot be synthesized, hospitals and patient care facilities depend upon blood supplied by human donors. The first blood bank was organized in this country in 1937, and since that time blood banks that collect, store, and regulate distribution of human blood have become an integral and necessary part of medical care.

Originally, blood banks were nonprofit organizations dependent upon voluntary donors. As the demand for blood increased, however, the voluntary blood banks often could not meet the need; hence "commercial" blood banks have developed. These banks usually pay the donor for his blood and charge the hospitals for the blood supplied. Today there are six commercial blood banks operating in North Carolina which supplement the voluntary banks. Nevertheless, most of the blood used in this state is still donated voluntarily.

The voluntary banks generally follow one of several patterns. Hospital blood banks are located within a hospital and supply blood only to that particular hospital. Some of these hospital blood banks participate in the Red Cross program and receive blood from a regional Red Cross blood center. The regional blood centers of the American Red Cross collect and distribute blood only to participating hospitals in a given region. Community blood banks also exist in North Carolina; under this arrangement a single blood bank serves all of the hospitals in the local area.

Patients receive blood by way of transfusion, which raises certain problems. A degree of risk accompanies a transfusion, and injury or untoward results can occur despite precautions. Recently, patients in civil litigations have tried to hold physicians, hospitals, blood banks, and even blood donors liable for the injuries sustained as a result of a transfusion. Such a claim might be brought in a suit upon any of

several bases. Perhaps the most common claim arises from a severe hemolitic transfusion reaction, commonly called an *incompatibility reaction*. This may occur when the patient is inadvertently transfused with a blood type other than his own. Such transfusion reactions are most frequently caused by technical or clerical errors in handling the transfused blood. Legal suits concerning such incompatibility reactions have generally sought to prove negligence on the part of those handling the blood.[1] In one North Carolina case, *Davis v. Wilson*,[2] a woman died as a result of being transfused during an operation with blood incompatible with her own. A medical technician in the hospital's own blood bank admitted making a clerical mistake in recording the patient's blood type and in mislabeling the pint of blood to be transfused. The Court ruled that the employer-hospital would be liable for the negligent acts of its employee-technician on the principle of respondent superior. The physicians who were associated with the hospital's laboratory department were not held liable for the technician's error; they were not her employers but rather her fellow employees.

Another type of complication that can arise from blood transfusions is an *allergic reaction*. These reactions are usually much less

1. Ward v. Orange Memorial Hospital Assn., 193 S2d 429 (Fla. App. 1967).
2. 265 N. C. 139, 143 S.E.2d 107 (1965).

serious than incompatibility reactions and they have not yet generated a significant amount of litigation.[3] In both allergic reactions and severe hemolytic transfusion reactions the blood transfused is "good blood"; it simply is incompatible to some degree with the patient's blood. .

A second set of complications involved in an increasing number of lawsuits stems from the transfusion of so-called "bad blood," or blood that contains and can transmit *diseases*. Three major diseases may be transmitted through transfusions: malaria, syphilis, and homologous serum hepatitis. Malaria and syphilis no longer present serious problems because they can easily be detected through routine tests on the blood, but the presence of homologous serum hepatitis in the transfusion blood presents one of the most difficult problems to the medical and legal professions today.

Though new techniques are being developed, no method of detecting the presence of the hepatitis virus in human blood which is sufficiently effective, practical, and economical to be widely accepted is now available. Legal and medical journals record many cases in which patients who received transfusions later developed hepatitis. In a number of states these patients are suing hospitals and blood banks in attempts to recover damages and compensation for the disease.

The question of hospital and blood bank liability for transmittal of disease may be resolved in favor of the patient on several different legal theories.[4] First, as in the in-

compatibility cases, plaintiffs have sought to recover for *negligence*. This allegation requires a plaintiff-patient to prove that the defendant-hospital or blood bank owed him a duty of care, that this duty was breached by the defendant's failure to act reasonably and exercise the necessary degree of care, and that the plaintiff sustained injury as a result of this negligence. Most of the plaintiffs who have relied solely on a cause of action in negligence have been unsuccessful. Since until recently no tests have been available to detect the hepatitis virus in donated blood, courts have not generally found blood banks and hospitals negligent for failing to detect it. Recently, however, some courts have looked more closely at the entire collection and transfusion process and have ruled that negligence may occur at any stage. In a 1967 Florida case,[5] a widow's suit for damages for her husband's death from hepatitis following a transfusion was allowed to proceed to trial on a theory of negligence. The court reasoned that though it may be impossible to detect or eliminate the hepatitis virus once the blood has been taken, a jury may find that the risk that the virus was present could have been reduced through greater care in screening the donors. A donor of one of the pints of blood transfused into the patient testified that he had not been asked any questions regarding previous diseases or his general health before the blood was taken. There was also evidence in that case that interviewing, screening, and selecting of donors were done by nonmedical and allegedly unqualified employees.

A second theory on which suits have been brought against the hospitals and blood banks is breach of an *express warranty*. Under this allegation a transfusion is considered to be the sale of a product, blood. Under the Uniform Commercial Code which governs sales

transactions in all fifty states, a seller may be liable for damages sustained by the buyer if the article fails to conform to express warranties stated by the seller. In blood transfusion cases, the patient would need to prove that express statements warranting the blood as pure were made to him by a doctor or hospital or blood bank employee. This is extremely difficult to do. Indeed, most pints of blood are labeled with written disclaimers of warranty, expressly stating that the blood may be impure and acknowledging the risk of hepatitis.

Many more cases have been based on the theory of breach of *implied warranties*. Under the Uniform Commercial Code, the law implies warranties of "fitness for use" (i.e., it is good for the intended use) and "merchantability" (i.e., it is generally a safe product) whenever a product is sold. If the blood is not "fit" for its intended use of transfusion, the seller may be liable. The New York case of *Perlmutter v. Beth David Hospital*[6] was the first leading case in which the plaintiff claimed a breach of implied warranties in the blood transfusion he received. The New York Court of Appeals reasoned that warranties were applicable only in cases involving sales contracts and that the relationship between the patient and hospital constituted an agreement for "service"—for care and treatment—not for the "sale" of specific products. The court stated:

The supplying of blood by the hospital was entirely subordinate to its paramount function of furnishing trained personnel and specialized facilities in an endeavor to restore plaintiff's health. It was not for blood — or iodine or bandages — for which plaintiff bargained, but . . . .to provide whatever medical treatment was considered advisable. The conclusion is evident that the furnishing of blood was only an incidental and very secondary adjunct to the services performed by the hospital, and therefore was not within the provisions of the Sales Act.[7]

Many other courts have followed the *Perlmutter* case, holding that a

3. In such cases plaintiffs have had difficulty proving permanent injury as a result of the transfusion. See Dorsey v. Knickerbocker Hospital, 271 N.Y.S.2d 727 (1966).

4. See: "Serum hepatitis through blood transfusions: a wrong without a remedy?" 24 Southwest L.R. 305 (1970); 38 Fordham L. Rev. 830 (1970); 46 North Dak. L. Rev. 367 (1970); Trout, "Blood Transfusions," 73 Dick. L. Rev. 201 (1969); Haut and Alter, Blood Transfusions—Strict Liability? 43 St. Johns L. Rev. 557 (1969); Van Meveren, The Extension of Liability to Service Contracts—Emphasizing the Furnishing of Unfit Blood for Transfusion, 6 Am. Bus. Law 517 (1968).

5. 196 So.2d 205 (Fla., 1967).

6. Hader v. Sayet, 308 N.Y. 100, 123 N.E. 2d 792 (1957).

7. Id.

blood transfusion is a service and not a sale.[8] Even in cases in which blood had been furnished by an independent blood bank and not a hospital the sale-service distinction has been upheld.[9] Law commentaries have been generally critical of the sale-service distinction, especially when applied to independent and commercial blood banks whose sole purpose is to collect and transfer blood for a monetary consideration. The courts have been reluctant to impose liability on either hospitals or blood banks, however, because of the improbability of detecting the presence of hepatitis in the donated blood. Such reluctance even led one court to characterize the blood transfusion as a *gift* rather than a sale.[10] Parallel to these court decisions, the legislatures in several states have declared that for warranty purposes, the transfer of blood is to be considered a service and not a sale.[11]

Recently several states have rejected the Perlmutter reasoning as an artificial distinction created to justify the court's public policy determination. As the court stated in *Russell v. Community Blood Bank:*

It seems to us a distortion to take what is, at least arguably a sale, twist it into the shape of a service, and then employ this transformed material in erecting the framework of a major policy decision.[12]

When the courts make reference to policy determinations, they indicate the basic question they are struggling with—who should bear

the burden of cost incurred by a patient who contracts hepatitis? In *Russell v. Community Blood Bank,* one concurring opinion indicated that this burden should be placed upon the blood bank:

It is more consonant with right and justice to require the Blood Bank to be held absolutely and *strictly* answerable to the consumers of its products for defects therein so that the burden . . . may be spread among all who benefit . . . rather than to require such losses to be borne by the innocent victims alone.[13]

The concept of holding the blood bank strictly liable became a legal precedent this past October in a case that is likely to be an extremely important and far-reaching decision in this area. In *Cunningham v. MacNeal Memorial Hospital*[14] the Illinois Supreme Court ruled that both hospitals and blood banks will be strictly liable to patients who contract post-transfusion hepatitis regardless of any negligence by the hospital or blood bank.

The theory of strict liability which has been developed and expanded in the courts in recent years imposes liability in the absence of negligence primarily for reasons of public policy. A generally accepted definition of strict liability is found in Section 402A of the Restatement (Second) of Torts, a treatise that has been a guide to courts and attorneys over the years:

(I) One who sells any product in a defective condition unreasonably dangerous to the user or consumer or to his property is subject to liability for physical harm thereby caused to the ultimate user or consumer, or to his property, (a) the seller is engaged in the business of selling such a product, and (b) it is expected to reach the user or consumer in the condition in which it is sold.
(II) The rule stated in subsection (I) applies although (a) the seller has exercised all possible care in the preparation and sale of his product, and (b) the user or consumer has not bought the product from or entered into any contractual relation with the seller.

To apply the theory of strict liability, it is necessary first to find that a blood transfusion constitutes a sale of a product. The Illinois court rejected the reasoning in the older *Perlmutter* case as "simply unrealistic" and found that both hospitals and blood banks were clearly within a commercial distribution chain to sell blood as a product.

The court also dismissed the hospital's argument that it should not be held strictly liable since the current state of medical science provides no means of detecting the existence of the serum hepatitis virus in whole blood. "To allow a defense to strict liability on the ground that there is no way, either practical or theoretical, for a defendant to ascertain the existence of impurities in the product would be to emasculate the doctrine and in a very real sense would signal a return to a negligence theory."[15] Thus, the court decided to place the entire financial burden for post-transfusion hepatitis on the institutional supplier rather than the innocent patient.

The practical effect of this decision is that hospitals and blood banks will have to purchase liability insurance coverage for transfusion-related disease. The insurance industry is expected to respond with new coverage; the premium is the question. Alternatively, legislation may be passed to alter the court's decision by statute.

While the legal implications are being pondered by blood bank administrators, researchers continue to seek a means of detecting the virus. Will that make the entire controversy moot? Probably not. Once an effective method of detection is discovered, should any blood bank or hospital be considered negligent which did not employ it? Or should reasonable cost be a factor? The Illinois court intimated that necessary costs could be absorbed by the hospital, which means passing it back to the patient.

8. Whitehurst v. American National Red Cross, 1 Ariz. App. 326, 402 P.2d 584 (1965); Stoneker v. St. Joseph's Hosp., 233 F. Supp. 105 (Col. 1964); Balkowitsch v. Minneapolis War Memorial Blood Bank, 270 Minn. 151, 123 N.W.2d 805 (1965); Koenig v. Milwaukee Blood Center, Inc., 23 Wis.2d 324, 127 N.W.2d 50 (1964).

9. Balkowitsch v. Minneapolis War Memorial Blood Bank, 270 Minn. 151, 123 N.W.2d 805 (1965).

10. Whitehurst v. American National Red Cross, 1 Ariz. App. 326, 402 P.2d 584 (1965).

11. ARIZ. REV. STAT. ANN. § 36-1151 (Supp. 1969); CAL. HEALTH AND SAFETY CODE § 1606 (West Supp. 1970); MASS. GEN. LAWS ANN. ch. 106 § 2-316(5) (Supp. 1970).

12. 185 So.2d 749, 752, (Fla. App. 1966). See also Community Blood Bank, Inc. v. Russell, 196 So.2d 115 (Fla. 1967); Jackson v. Muhlenberg Hospital, 53 N.J. 138, 249 A.2d (1969); Carter v. Inter-Faith Hospital of Queens, 60 Misc.2d 793, 304 N.Y.S.2d 97 (1969).

13. Community Blood Bank, Inc. v. Russell, 196 So.2d 115, 121 (Fla. 1967).
14. Cunningham v. MacNeal Memorial Hospital, ——— N.E.2d ——— (Ill., 1970).

15. Id.

In North Carolina the Supreme Court has never decided the question of liability for transfusion-induced hepatitis. However, several bills will probably be introduced into the 1971 General Assembly dealing with the subject. Two bills that have been proposed would declare by statute that any transfusion or transplantation shall be considered a service and not a sale. This would eliminate the possibility that North Carolina courts would adopt implied warranty or strict liability theories. However, one of the proposed bills also requires all persons who are engaged in rendering the service of transfusion or transplantation to exercise the "highest degree of care," a standard which is more stringent than the normally applied "reasonable degree of care." This latter bill would also make it the defendant's duty to prove that he exercised the highest degree of care, rather than make the plaintiff-patient prove he did not. Thus the bill prohibits adoption of the strict liability and warranties theories, but requires greater care than under the traditional negligence theory.

Another proposed bill would require all blood-banking operations to take place only at the direction and under the supervision of a physician licensed in North Carolina. Violation of the statute would constitute a misdemeanor. The bill would also stipulate that due care must be exercised to minimize the risks of transmitting the agents that might cause hepatitis and other diseases by careful selection and screening of prospective blood donors. This seems simply to be a codification of the present law and would not be persuasive in the court's decision whether to follow Illinois' strict liability.

It is difficult to predict the outcome of legislative action on this matter in North Carolina. Predicting how North Carolina courts will rule on the liability question is equally difficult. However, the question will most certainly continue to be important and an overriding concern of physicians, administrators, and others in the blood bank or transfusion business until an effective, practical, and economical method of screening the hepatitis virus from blood is discovered and made available.

Removal of Judges   (Continued from Page 10)

options of resigning or of retiring voluntarily if he was otherwise qualified for retirement compensation.

Subject to certain fundamental safeguards, the Standards Commission would be free to establish its own procedures. Commission action would be initiated by signed complaint of any citizen, or by Commission investigation on its own motion. Complaints having some basis would be investigated, and those found to be substantiated but of a minor nature would usually be terminated by communication with the judge concerned. Major violations of judicial standards—which experience again has shown to be quite rare—would proceed through the investigatory stage to an offer of a due process hearing to the repondent judge. If the findings of the Commission supported the allegations, the Commission could recommend censure, retirement, or removal to the Supreme Court.

The Commission would have authority to initiate investigations on its own motion to take care of instances of alleged misconduct of a substantial nature for which there were no complainants. Widespread and persistent rumors, for example, should be investigated for the good of the profession as well as the protection of the individual judge. An example would be newspaper reports of misconduct, which, if not investigated and acted on, might do enormous damage to the image of the judge and public respect for the administration of justice generally.

The Commission would be authorized to administer oaths and to punish for contempt and compel the attendance of witnesses and the production of documents. Its proceedings would be confidential until such time as it made its final recommendations to the Supreme Court. This provision is vital, as allegations of misconduct are frequently groundless, and judges under investigation are entitled to this protection until such time as the charges are found to be supported. Public confidence in the integrity of the courts is also at stake here; it should not be shaken without reason. Further, confidentiality is essential to protect complainants and witnesses, many of whom would be reluctant to complain or testify for fear of publicity or reprisal. Of course, if the respondent judge chose to waive the privilege of confidentiality, he could do so. Detailed regulations in this field should be left to the Commission.

Four of the seven members of the Commission should concur in any recommendation to censure or remove any justice or judge, and a majority of all members of the Supreme Court must concur in any censure or removal order, or in an order to take no action (dismiss) the proceedings. Any justice or judge would, of course, be disqualified from acting in any case in which he was a respondent.

HOW DO WE
MEASURE
THE PROBLEM OF
JUVENILE JUSTICE
IN NORTH CAROLINA?

By Mason P. Thomas, Jr.
and Katherine A. Yost

The National Picture

Reliable statistical data on the extent of delinquency and neglect in the United States are difficult or impossible to obtain.

Juvenile statistics on a national level have been collected over the years by two federal agencies—the Federal Bureau of Investigation and the Children's Bureau of the U.S. Department of Health, Education, and Welfare, which has been replaced by the Office of Juvenile Delinquency and Youth Development. The FBI *Uniform Crime Reports* are based on *arrest* reports voluntarily submitted by law enforcement agencies throughout the United States. These records do not reflect actual court dispositions or adjudications of delinquency, nor do they show the number of children who are handled informally by law enforcement agencies without an official referral to the juvenile court by petition. (These informal encounters are estimated to be about half the police contacts with children.) The data from the Office of Juvenile Delinquency and Youth Development on the number of juvenile delinquency *cases* are based on a national sample of juvenile courts drawn from the Current Population Survey sample of the Bureau of the Census, which is intended to be representative of the country as a whole.

Since the age jurisdiction of the juvenile court varies significantly from state to state, the delinquency figures available from either source have limited value. They show trends, but they do not document the extent of the problem in the United States. Both types of data, police arrests of juveniles reported by the FBI and juvenile court delinquency cases reported by HEW, show a similarity in trends over the last twenty years. The trends have been steadily upward since 1949, except for 1961. In 1968, the reported increases were similar under both methods — 9.7 per cent in police arrests of juveniles, 10.7 per cent in delinquency court cases. Neither method of reporting juvenile delinquency statistics would show the incidence of juvenile in-volvement in which the offense is not reported or the child not apprehended.[1]

In 1966, there were some 900,000 juvenile delinquency cases (excluding traffic offenses) that involved 774,000 children (some children were in juvenile court more than once during the year). These children represent 2.5 per cent of all children aged 10 through 17 in the United States. Between 1960 and 1968, the number of juvenile cases increased by 76.4 per cent compared with a 24.5 per cent increase in the 10-17 age group in the population of the United States.[2]

It is estimated that one in every nine children will be referred to juvenile court for delinquency before his eighteenth birthday. The estimate for boys is one in six, since they are more frequently involved in delinquency than girls.[3]

1. OFFICE OF JUVENILE DELINQUENCY AND YOUTH DEVELOPMENT, U.S. DEPARTMENT OF HEALTH, EDUCATION, AND WELFARE, JUVENILE COURT STATISTICS—1968 (Stat. Ser. No. 95), at 1.
2. Ibid.
3. CHILDREN'S BUREAU, U.S. DEPARTMENT OF HEALTH, EDUCATION, AND WELFARE, JUVENILE COURT STATISTICS—1964 (Stat. Ser. No. 83), at 1.

The FBI arrest figures for 1969 (excluding traffic offenders) show that 39 per cent of those arrested were under 21 and 26 per cent were less than 18. The percentage of youth arrests was higher in urban areas, where 63 per cent of all persons arrested were less than 25. The FBI arrest figures indicate that youth arrests are escalating at a rate four times faster than their percentage increase in the national population.[4]

Another approach to evaluating the size of the national juvenile delinquency picture is through self-report studies in which samples of youth are asked about their own delinquent acts. One study revealed that 90 per cent of all youth admit to behavior that could have brought them within the jurisdiction of the juvenile court. Many of these offenses are noncriminal and would not be considered an offense among adults—running away from home, being unmanageable, violating curfews, etc.[5]

The North Carolina Picture

North Carolina has no law requiring that any state agency collect and analyze data on the extent of juvenile delinquency in the state. The State Department of Social Services is the only state agency that attempts to collect statewide data on juvenile cases. It receives reports on juvenile cases from county departments of social services (who provide juvenile probation services) and from some family counselors, who provide juvenile probation services in urban counties. No statewide figures are available concerning police arrests of juveniles.

Social service workers and family counselors make reports voluntarily to the State Department of Social Services using juvenile court cards furnished by the U.S. Department of Health, Education, and Welfare. The State Department of Social Services in turn reports on

juvenile cases for the State of North Carolina to the Office of Juvenile Delinquency and Youth Development at the federal level.

There are great gaps and deficiencies in the available data for several reasons. The primary one is that reporting juvenile cases to any state agency is not mandatory but solely voluntary. In the 1969 figures, five counties did not report any court cases, and several others sent data covering only part of the year. Other reasons for the insufficiency of the 1969 data listed by the Social Services Department include (1) absence of a uniform system of reporting; (2) the inadequacy of the 1919 juvenile court law in defining categories of juvenile jurisdiction; (3) insufficient staff in the counties to make the reports; and (4) the transitional period during which only part of the state was under the district court system.[6]

Juvenile Court Cases

In 1969, 6,807 court cases involving juveniles were reported in North Carolina. Table I shows the types of cases included in the figure.

The data were reported for cases rather than for individual children. Many children were involved in two or more cases during the year; therefore the number of children actually represented by the data is somewhat smaller than the number of cases.

The data for North Carolina show that in 1969 slightly more than eight children per 1,000 between the ages of seven and 16 in the general population were reported as having been involved in court action for delinquency. Earlier analyses of delinquency data in North Carolina generally reported slightly more than three children per 1,000 involved in delinquency in the 0-16 age group.[7]

The ratio of boys to girls in the 1969 delinquency cases, including

traffic offenses, is less than three to one—3,897 to 1,326.[8] An earlier study (1963) reported a four-to-one boy-girl ratio. This suggests a trend toward greater involvement in delinquency among girls in North Carolina.

According to the available data, the number of cases in which white children were involved increased by 6.7 per cent from 1967 to 1969 while the comparable figure for nonwhite children showed an increase of 25.4 per cent.[9]

The most frequent reasons for referring boys as delinquent were charges of larceny and truancy, followed by burglary, vandalism, and ungovernable behavior. Among girls the most frequent reasons for referral were charges of truancy, ungovernable behavior, and running away.[10]

Table I
Number and Types of Juvenile Court Hearings, 1969

Delinquency	5,031
Traffic	192
Neglect	662
Abuse	106
Special Proceedings	816
TOTAL HEARINGS	6,807

* Includes custody controversies, consent to marry, etc.

Law Enforcement Figures

No statewide police juvenile arrest statistics are available. Individual police departments maintain a variety of records involving young people. For example, in 1969 in Charlotte 2,835 juveniles (under 16) were processed through the Youth Bureau. Of this number, 1,225 or 43 per cent were referred to juvenile court. Juveniles accounted for 13.4 per cent of all 1969 criminal arrests in Charlotte.[11] In Greensboro during this same 1969 period, 1,551 juveniles were arrested; of that number, 699 or 45 per cent were referred to the juvenile court. In both cities ap-

---

4. 1969 FBI UNIFORM CRIME REPORTS 33.
5. PRESIDENT'S COMMISSION ON LAW ENFORCEMENT AND ADMINISTRATION OF JUSTICE, CHALLENGE OF CRIME IN A FREE SOCIETY, 1967, at 55.

6. NORTH CAROLINA DEPARTMENT OF SOCIAL SERVICES, JUVENILE COURT CASES—1969, at 10.
7. Id. at 5.

8. Id. at 6.
9. Ibid.
10. Id. at 7.
11. Youth Aid Bureau, Charlotte Police Department, Annual Report, 1969.

proximately 81 per cent of the juveniles involved were males. In Greensboro 1,553 juveniles were handled last year (1970), of whom 631 or 41 per cent were referred to juvenile court.[12]

Detention

The State Department of Social Services collects data from two sources on the number of children involved in juvenile cases who were detained overnight in jails or juvenile detention homes. The data contained on juvenile court cards submitted through county departments and family counselors indicated that most of the delinquents arrested in 1969 were taken or allowed to return to their own homes, since these reports show that no overnight detention was made in 82.7 per cent of the reported juvenile cases. These data indicate that most of the children who were detained (17.3 per cent of all children involved in juvenile cases) were placed in approved county detention homes or licensed foster family homes under the supervision of the county department of social service. According to the juvenile court cards, 613 children were detained in detention homes, 279 were placed in foster family homes, and 182 held in jails or police stations during 1969.[13]

Another division of the State Department of Social Services (Division of Jail and Detention Services) receives reports from local jails and juvenile detention homes which gives a different picture. These data show that 1,207 children less than sixteen years of age were confined in the local jails of the state during 1969. According to the monthly reports submitted by the detention homes, 2,987 juveniles were detained in 1969.[14] North

Carolina has no state-supported detention homes for delinquent children. Seven counties (Buncombe, Durham, Forsyth, Gaston, Guilford, Mecklenburg, and Wake), each located in an urban area, have juvenile detention homes with a combined capacity of 114 beds. The homes are supported entirely with county tax funds. The average length of stay in them is about seven days.

Training Schools

The combined capacity of North Carolina's eight juvenile training schools is approximately 2,100 and the average length of stay within the system is twelve months. The schools stay full but at present there is no waiting list. During fiscal year 1969-70, there were 1,692 new admissions and 333 children were returned to the schools for violation of conditional release. (Conditional release is the technical term for after-care supervision). During the same period, 1,550 children left the schools on conditional release and 323 were discharged.[15]

According to the *Biennial Report of the North Carolina Board of Juvenile Corrections, 1964-66*, approximately *90 per cent* of the juveniles confined to training schools "make good" when they return to their own communities.[16] This remarkable claim has been omitted from later biennial reports. Statistics concerning the number of juveniles who "graduate" to adult criminal courts are not now available, however prison officials estimate that one in three to five persons committed to prison has a prior juvenile court record.[17] The number of children on probation statewide is also not now available.

Conclusion

North Carolina has established a separate juvenile justice system for children less than sixteen years of age which operates in different ways from place to place within the state. A few local governments have established specialized youth bureaus in their police departments, but no statewide information is available on the number of police contacts with delinquents or concerning how police discretion is used in North Carolina to provide services or referrals to other community agencies or to initiate a petition to bring the child within the juvenile jurisdiction of the district court. While many juvenile cases are reported voluntarily to the State Department of Social Services, many others go unreported because of the lack of a legal requirement to report. The Administrative Office of the Courts keeps certain statistics on the number of cases heard in the district courts of the state, but this data does not show the number of juvenile cases or what happened to the children involved in 1970. The Board of juvenile Correction keeps statistics for its own purposes, but these data are not adequate to show how many children are rehabilitated by their training school experiences. The Department of Correction keeps information concerning the juveniles that come within the prison system, but again the information is sketchy and inadequate.

In short, we lack information about what is going on in juvenile corrections in North Carolina. Without adequate information, the effectiveness of the system cannot be evaluated nor whether the system achieves desirable goals determined. The juvenile corrections system involves a number of agencies of state and local government who do not necessarily work together toward the best interests of the children involved in the system.

12. Youth Division, Greensboro Police Dept. Annual Report, 1970.
13. North Carolina Department of Social Services, op. cit, supra note 6 at 15.
14. Department of Social Services, Division of Jail and Detention Services, Reports, Detention Home Populations, January through December, 1969 (Raleigh, mimeo.).
15. Personal communication with Mr. Charles Bennett, Administrative Assistant, Board of Juvenile Correction, January 18, 1971.
16. NORTH CAROLINA BOARD OF JUVENILE CORRECTION, BIENNIAL REPORT, 1964-1966, at 6.
17. Personal communication with Mr. Charles Wilson, Research Director, Department of Correction, January 18, 1971.

This article will appear as a chapter in the senior author's book in process, Juvenile Corrections in North Carolina.

JAILS

(Continued from Page 15)

confined in jails during the past fiscal year. We still have too many people having to wait over 30 days in jail to be tried and therefore causing crowded conditions. There are entirely too many mental cases being confined at least temporarily in jail.

Our interpretation of the jail legislation enacted by the 1967 General Assembly is that it was designed to improve jails in North Carolina, not to close them. We believe in working with local officials to this end, and a jail will be closed only when there is no other possible solution.

We are sure, however, that with the outstanding cooperation evidenced in the past two years, the next two years will show even greater improvement.

Health Care *(Continued from Page 5)*

nurse who dispenses band-aids and aspirin and doubles as a truant officer. I think we can do better. We can also do better in terms of industrial health programs, particularly programs of health care organized around family groups identified with given industries.

I mentioned county and district health departments as a neglected source of improved and increased health care. I submit that it is a function of government, in health as in other areas, to guarantee those essential public services that are not otherwise provided. As our concern for improved health services turns toward the organization of systems of care, we must be guided toward public mechanisms and agencies that are already charged with responsibilities for health care. Universities and their medical schools are enormously important—but they are not sufficient unto themselves to solve our problems of medical care. We do not look to schools of law to solve our problems of law and order; nor can we expect medical schools and universities to solve all problems in health care. We need look to those agencies charged with the public responsibility to improve health services, and we need to expand their mechanisms and mandates.

"Solutions to health problems do not follow automatically from establishing medical centers, producing more health personnel, and enlarging health services. There are certain critical connections between medical technology and the public, and if these connections are not firm and effective the benefits of that technology do not reach the public." [Ibid.] Some state will one day authorize and fund a health service plan—hopefully pluralistic, hopefully flexible, hopefully under local authority, and hopefully sensitive to the needs of both frustrated consumers and well-intentioned, dedicated professionals. It might be North Carolina.

THE PROPOSED CONSOLIDATION OF
CHARLOTTE AND MECKLENBURG COUNTY

By Warren J. Wicker

On March 22, 1971, voters of Mecklenburg County will vote in a referendum on the proposed consolidation of the City of Charlotte and Mecklenburg County, following over forty years of discussion about their consolidation. If they approve, enactment of a charter for the new government and other companion legislation will be secured from the 1971 General Assembly now in session. If they approve, the new government, to be known as The Consolidated Government of Charlotte and Mecklenburg County, will be officially established on August 15, 1972. At that time the City of Charlotte will be abolished and the powers and functions of both the Charlotte government and the County government will be merged into the new one.

The County also has five smaller municipalities: Cornelius, Davidson, Huntersville, Matthews, and Pineville. If the voters approve consolidation of Charlotte and Mecklenburg County on March 22, each of these towns will conduct a referendum within 120 days thereafter to decide whether it will also merge with the consolidated government or continue as a separate municipality. Whatever their choice, citizens of the smaller towns will be citizens of the consolidated government—just as they are now citizens of Mecklenburg County.

This article reviews the background to the current consolidation effort in Mecklenburg County and the work of the Charter Commission that developed the plan and describes briefly the proposed plan of consolidated government.

Background

The governments of Charlotte and Mecklenburg County have been closely related since their very beginnings and have a long history of cooperative relationships. The first major move toward consolidation came in 1927 when Miss Carrie McLean, a General Assembly member from Mecklenburg County, introduced legislation to enable all local governments in Mecklenburg County to merge into one.[1] The plan would have extended the boundaries of the City of Charlotte to those of the County and made the City the single local government in the county. The existing county government and those of the smaller towns would have been eliminated. A vote on the plan was to

<hr>

1. Ch. 192, N.C. Pvt. Laws of 1927.

be held and the plan was to take effect under a petition procedure.

An adequate petition was never secured and no action under the legislation was taken. In fact, Representative McLean apparently did not actually anticipate any. According to newspaper accounts, she thought that consolidation would soon be needed, that many municipal services were needed throughout the county, that one government could serve the people more efficiently than could many, and she introduced the legislation as a means of promoting discussion of consolidation and work toward it.

Cooperative action in a number of areas continued, and in 1949 and 1950 a major study looking toward consolidation was undertaken.[2] This study did not produce a charter, nor was any vote on consolidation held. But the work did give impetus to more cooperative activity and functional mergers. The public schools, the tax collection offices, and the health departments were merged in the following years. Cooperative actions in law enforcement and water and sewerage were expanded. Other activities were also consolidated later, in part as the result of this study and in part from the continuing interest in more efficient and convenient arrangements. In 1953 legislation was secured that authorized the City and the County to merge any of their departments for the purpose of providing "more economical administration."[3]

In effect, the current effort started in 1967, when the Charlotte Chamber of Commerce created a special Single Government Study Committee with President Grier Martin of Davidson College as chairman. The Committee's report, *Single Government*, was issued by the Chamber in early 1968. The report analyzed the current arrangements and found that of all the expenditures of the City and County governments, 57 percent were already expended through consolidated departments; another 13 percent were for purposes the Committee felt were needed only in the City; and the remaining 30 percent represented areas of expenditures where joint or consolidated administration were judged to be needed. Clearly, the Committee observed, consolidation was already much further along in Mecklenburg than many people realized—more than in most metropolitan areas of the country. Because of the common needs, the shared interests, the need for better coordination of all services, and in order to make government more representative, the Committee suggested several immediate steps and recommended that full consolidation be achieved by 1973.

One of its recommendations was that a special committee be appointed by the governing boards of the county to draft legislation creating a charter commission. That committee was appointed and was headed by Brodie S. Griffith, associate publisher of the *Charlotte Observer*. The Griffith committee proposed a charter commission of fifteen, plus a chairman and the mayor of Charlotte and the chairman of the Mecklenburg Board of County Commissioners, who would serve ex officio without a vote. Five members were to be appointed by the mayor of Charlotte, with the approval of the Council; five by the chairman of the Board of County Commissioners, with the approval of the Board; and one each by the mayors of the smaller towns with the approval of their governing boards. The chairman was to be appointed jointly by the mayor of Charlotte and the chairman of the Board of County Commissioners. The plan also called for a Citizens' Review Committee of 50 persons to provide wide community representation in developing the consolidation plan. Members of the Review Committee were to be appointed in the same fashion, and in the same proportions, as the members of the charter commission. The committee also recommended a single county-wide vote on the merger of Charlotte and Mecklenburg County, to be followed by the votes in the smaller towns noted above.

The Griffith committee recommendations were embodied in legislation that was approved by the 1969 General Assembly.[4]

Charter Commission

The members of the Charlotte-Mecklenburg Charter Commission and its Citizens' Review Committee were appointed in the spring of 1969 and the Commission held its organizational meeting on May 19, 1969. The chairman of the Charter Commission is Jones Y. Pharr, Jr., prominent businessman, civic leader, chairman of the ABC Board, and a member of the county school board when the City and County schools were merged. Other members of the Commission are:

Fred D. Alexander, member of the City Council and real estate man
G. Randolph Babcock, businessman and former city councilman
Mrs. Louise Brennan, county chairman of the Democratic Party
Dr. Elizabeth Corkey, public health administrator
Jack Crump, Pineville town manager
Roy T. Fortner, Huntersville businessman
Charles H. Funderburk, U.S. Post Office, Matthews
Joseph W. Grier, attorney and former chairman of a Charlotte charter revision committee

2. The Institute of Government made the study at the request of the city and county governing boards.
3. Ch. 742, N.C. Session Laws of 1953.
4. Ch. 67, N.C. Session Laws of 1969.

Arthur H. Jones, banker and member of the General Assembly
William H. McEniry, Vice-Chancellor, UNC-C
Wallace S. Osborne, attorney and former member of the Board of County Commissioners
Reitzel Snider, insurance broker
William I. Ward, Jr., counsel, Duke Power Company
J. E. Wayland, minister
John M. Belk, mayor of Charlotte, and Dr. James G. Martin, chairman of the Mecklenburg Board of County Commissioners, serve ex officio.[5]

Work Schedule of the Commission

Funds for the Charter Commission's work under the legislation establishing it were provided in equal shares by Charlotte and Mecklenburg County. The Commission contracted with the Institute of Government to undertake the principal research and draft the charter. It also retained a small staff in Charlotte to direct activities on the scene, provide information to the public, and handle arrangements for the Commission and its committees.[6]

The Commission spent its first six months in background studies of (1) government in Charlotte, Mecklenburg County, and North Carolina, and (2) the approaches and experiences with reorganization of government in metropolitan areas throughout the country.

Commission representatives visited Nashville, Jacksonville, Baton Rouge, and Indianapolis to examine arrangements of those governments. Background seminars, covering the nature of metropolitan governments and looking at specific attempts at consolidation (both successful and unsuccessful) were held in Charlotte for members of the Commission, the Citizens' Review Committee, and officials of the seven governments.

Early in its work the Commission declared that its principal goal was to develop a plan of government that would be representative of all citizens and provide fair taxation for all taxpayers. All meetings of the Commission were open to the public, and great effort was made to involve as many citizens as possible in developing the plan. News media provided regular and extensive coverage of the Commission's work.

Almost 100 special reports and memoranda, covering all functions and activities of the various

5. Charles M. Lowe was chairman of the Board of Commissioners when the Charter Commission was organized and served on the Commission until his retirement as chairman of the Board of County Commissioners in December, 1969.
6. The author served as director for the Charter Commission. David M. Lawrence and H. Rutherford Turnbull, III, assistant directors of the Institute of Government, were principally responsible for drafting the charter. L. M. Wright, Jr., editorial writer for the Charlotte Observer and a member of a number of previous metropolitan study groups, took a leave of absence from the Observer to serve as associate director for the Commission.

governments and special questions or problems, were prepared by the staff, special consultants, and officials of the governments for the Commission.

Most of these reports and memoranda were reviewed initially by one of the five committees into which the Commission divided itself and by members of the Citizens' Review Committee. Afterward, the reports and the conclusions of the committees were reviewed by the full Commission as it developed the plan of government and the charter.

Public hearings were held on all functions and activities and on numerous other questions: the basic structure of the government, community participation, composition of the governing board, and similar questions.

The public hearings and the committee work occurred largely from Fall, 1969, to September, 1970, overlapping the drafting of the charter for the new government. The drafting procedure began in May, 1970, and was completed in February of 1971 (the time of this writing). The first draft of the charter was completed in early October, 1970. Between that time and January 26, 1971, the Commission held numerous review sessions and public hearings and completed its work on the charter, except for changes in the allocation of ABC revenues and sales tax receipts that were made on February 19, 1971.

The Commission's work is reflected in two documents. Its report, *Responsible, Responsive Government*, outlines how the Commission went about its work, lists all the reports and studies completed, describes the existing governmental arrangements in Mecklenburg County and the plan for the proposed consolidated government, and gives the reasons for the Commission's recommendations. A second document, *The Proposed Charter for the Consolidated Government of Charlotte and Mecklenburg County*, contains the full text of both the charter and companion legislation necessary to establish the consolidated government.[7]

The Plan of Consolidation

The proposed plan of government draws heavily on existing patterns but also includes a number of significant modifications. The existing governments of Charlotte and Mecklenburg County are council-manager governments. So, also, are the governments of Pineville and Huntersville. Cornelius, Davidson, and Matthews operate under a mayor-council plan in which the mayor's position is structurally a "weak" one.

7. Limited numbers of copies of some of the reports to the Commission and of the Commission's publications are available from the Commission, 400 East Second Street, Charlotte, N.C. 28201. Information and copies of some of the reports may also be secured from the Institute of Government.

The proposed consolidated government is termed by the Commission as a council-mayor-administrator form. Its chief elements are a combination of those found in the council-manager and strong-mayor–council plans.

Council. The proposed Council will have eighteen members, elected to four-year staggered terms on a partisan basis. Twelve members are to be elected from single-member districts and six are to be elected at large. (All governing board members in the county are now elected at large for two-year terms with no provisions for staggering. All municipal elections are nonpartisan; county commissioners are elected on a partisan basis.)

All legislative powers previously vested in the county and municipal governing boards are vested in the Council. In addition, the power of the Council to make appointments has been increased. The Council appoints all the semi-independent operating boards and commissions except the Hospital Authority, and it will decide how all appointments are made to committees created by the Council.

Mayor. The mayor will also be elected to a four-year term, by a county-wide vote, in partisan elections. It is anticipated that he will serve full-time. His initial salary will be $36,000.

The mayor is the chief executive and heads the general consolidated administration—all functions and activities not vested by law in a particular office or under the direction of one of the semi-independent boards and commissions. The mayor is responsible for recommending the budget to the Council, presides over the Council, and has a veto over most Council actions, including an item veto on appropriations. The mayor appoints the chief administrative officer and four other department heads, with Council approval, and approves the appointment of the police and fire chiefs by the Council and all department heads appointed by the chief administrative officer. In addition, the mayor may call conferences of the chairmen of the semi-independent boards and commissions, their executive heads, and department heads of the general government. He thus has considerably more formal strength than either the mayor of Charlotte or the chairman of the Board of County Commissioners now has, but less than most "strong mayors" in the country's larger cities. For example, most strong mayors have much more extensive powers of appointment, both of administrative personnel and to boards and commissions, than the recommended plan calls for.

Chief Administrative Officer. The chief administrative officer is given extensive powers by the charter, but fewer than managers typically have in council-manager governments. He is appointed by the mayor, with Council approval, and may be removed by the mayor alone. He reports to the mayor and not to the Council, as he does in the council-manager plan. He has, however, administrative and appointive powers over the general consolidated administration substantially like those of a manager. The mayor must approve his appointments of department heads, but he alone removes them. All other employees (except those covered by some form of civil service or employees of the semi-independent boards and commissions) are appointed by the CAO and may be removed by him.

Administrative Organization. Another distinctive feature of the proposed plan, as compared with other city-county consolidations in recent years, is that the organization of the general consolidated administration is not structured by the charter. The charter and general law do impose particular duties and responsibilities on particular officers—tax supervisor, finance director, planning director, and others—but the general administrative structure is not specified in the charter. Both the original structure and the reorganization of the administrative structure are left to the discretion of the mayor and the Council. The charter provides that the mayor may propose plans of administrative organization that go into effect when approved by the Council, or, if the Council takes no action, after ninety days. If the Council disapproves a plan, the mayor then submits another until he develops one that the Council will approve.

The initial administrative organization will be that in existence on the day of consolidation—and this arrangement will continue until modified as described above.

School Board. Public schools in Mecklenburg County are already consolidated. The school board is composed of nine members elected to six-year staggered terms on a nonpartisan basis. The schools are a fiscally dependent agency. The county commissioners levy the local taxes for the support of the schools.

The proposed plan continues the general arrangements for the schools without change. The school board will relate to the consolidated governing board as it now relates to the board of county commissioners. The manner in which the school board is to be elected is changed in the proposed plan. This plan calls for six members to be elected from districts (two Council districts in each school district) and three at large, the same ratio between district and at-large election as for the Council. Members will continue to be elected on a nonpartisan basis, but their terms, which continue staggered, have been shortened to four years.

Boards and Commissions. Ten functions continue to be the responsibility of semi-independent boards and commissions. These are public health, social services, Auditorium-Coliseum, public housing, library, parks and recreation, redevelopment, hospitals, veterans recreation, and drainage. Almost all of these activities, while separate from the general consolidated administration, have been more fully integrated with the general government than they now are. Most will be subject to general personnel policies, fiscal control, and budgeting procedures. All will be subject to

the mandatory referral procedures of the planning process, and all are subject to conferences called by the mayor and the CAO.

The composition of most of the boards has been changed to assure that they are representative of the entire county.

Advisory Boards. All the existing advisory boards—community facilities, mental health, airport, cemetery, model neighborhood, community relations and the like—are continued without change. These are established under ordinances or resolutions of the present governments and may be changed by the Council in the future as it determines.

Technical and Regulatory Agencies. A number of these now exist under either ordinances of the existing governments, charter, or general law. Examples are the Board of Adjustment, Firemen's Relief Board of Trustees, Electrical Advisory Board, Law Enforcement Pension Fund, and the Boxing and Wrestling Commission. All have been continued with only those changes necessary to conform their structures and manner of selection to the new government.

State-Local Agencies. In this classification are the ABC Board, elections, medical examiner, agricultural extension, community college, and jury commission. Only the necessary conforming changes are proposed with respect to these agencies. They will continue to have the same responsibilities and will relate to the consolidated government as they now relate to the Mecklenburg County government.

Elective Offices. In addition to the governing board members noted above, three county officers are now elected by the people: the sheriff, the register of deeds, and the county treasurer. Under the plan, the sheriff and the register of deeds will be elected as they now are and will exercise the same duties and responsibilities they now have. The office of county treasurer is changed to consolidated treasurer and will be filled by appointment by the CAO.

Financing Plan. The basic principle in financing is that services and functions will be financed by those receiving their benefits, or within the jurisdiction in which they are provided. The two-tier arrangement found in other consolidated governments is proposed. Some services and functions will be provided county-wide, and these will be supported from county-wide taxation or revenues that will be allocated to the county-wide part of the budget. Other services or functions will be provided only in "urban service districts" or will be provided at a higher level within these districts. These additional, or higher levels, of service will

PROPOSED ORGANIZATION FOR THE CONSOLIDATED GOVERNMENT OF CHARLOTTE AND MECKLENBURG COUNTY

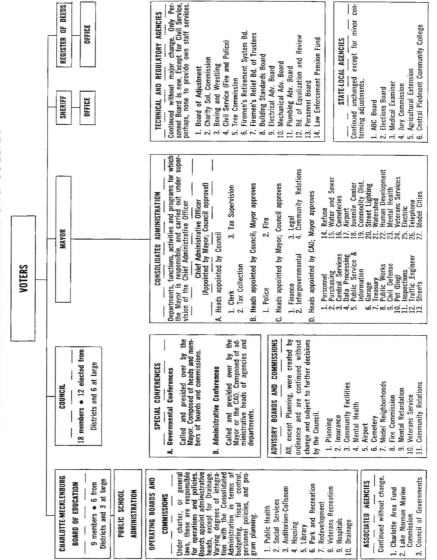

VOTERS

COUNCIL — 18 members • 12 elected from Districts and 6 at large

MAYOR

SHERIFF OFFICE

REGISTER OF DEEDS OFFICE

CHARLOTTE-MECKLENBURG BOARD OF EDUCATION
9 members • 6 from Districts and 3 at large

PUBLIC SCHOOL ADMINISTRATION

OPERATING BOARDS AND COMMISSIONS

Under charter, or general laws, these are responsible for operations and policies. Boards appoint administrative heads, except for Drainage. Varying degrees of integration with the Consolidated Administration in terms of budgeting, fiscal control, personnel policies, and program planning.

1. Public Health
2. Social Services
3. Auditorium-Coliseum
4. Housing
5. Library
6. Park and Recreation
7. Redevelopment
8. Veterans Recreation
9. Hospitals
10. Drainage

ASSOCIATED AGENCIES

Continued without change.

1. Charlotte Area Fund
2. Lake Norman Marine Commission
3. Council of Governments

SPECIAL CONFERENCES

A. Governmental Conferences

Called and presided over by the Mayor. Composed of heads and members of boards and commissions.

B. Administrative Conferences

Called and presided over by the Mayor or the CAO. Composed of administrative heads of agencies and departments.

ADVISORY BOARDS AND COMMISSIONS

All, except Planning, were created by ordinance and are continued without change and subject to further decisions by the Council.

1. Planning
2. Insurance
3. Community Facilities
4. Mental Health
5. Airport
6. Cemetery
7. Model Neighborhoods
8. Fire Commission
9. Mental Retardation
10. Veterans Service
11. Community Relations

CONSOLIDATED ADMINISTRATION

Departments, functions, activities and programs for which the Mayor is responsible, and carried out under supervision of the Chief Administrative Officer

Chief Administrative Officer
(Appointed by Mayor; Council approval)

A. Heads appointed by Council

1. Clerk
2. Tax Collection
3. Tax Supervision

B. Heads appointed by Council; Mayor approves

1. Police
2. Fire

C. Heads appointed by Mayor; Council approves

1. Finance
2. Intergovernmental
3. Legal
4. Community Relations

D. Heads appointed by CAO; Mayor approves

1. Personnel
2. Purchasing
3. Central Services
4. Data Processing
5. Public Service & Information
6. Garage
7. Treasury
8. Public Works
9. Civil Defense
10. Pet (Dog)
11. Inspections
12. Traffic Engineer
13. Streets
14. Refuse
15. Water and Sewer
16. Cemeteries
17. Airport
18. Juvenile Center
19. Commodity Dist.
20. Street Lighting
21. Watershed
22. Human Development
23. Mental Health
24. Veterans Services
25. Electric
26. Telephone
27. Model Cities

TECHNICAL AND REGULATORY AGENCIES

Continued without major change. Only Personnel Board is new. Except for Civil Service, perhaps, none to provide own staff services.

1. Board of Adjustment
2. Charity Sol. Commission
3. Boxing and Wrestling
4. Civil Service (Fire and Police)
5. Tree Commission
6. Firemen's Retirement System Bd.
7. Firemen's Relief Bd. of Trustees
8. Building Standards Board
9. Electrical Adv. Board
10. Mechanical Adv. Board
11. Plumbing Adv. Board
12. Bd. of Equalization and Review
13. Personnel Board
14. Law Enforcement Pension Fund

STATE-LOCAL AGENCIES

Continued unchanged except for minor conforming adjustments.

1. ABC Board
2. Elections Board
3. Medical Examiner
4. Jury Commission
5. Agricultural Extension
6. Central Piedmont Community College

be financed from revenues and taxes of the urban service districts.

The plan does not allocate functions between urban service districts and county-wide, or general service districts—a marked difference from the arrangements found in the city-county consolidations of recent years. The consolidated Council is free to make allocations each year as it determines best. Some revenues, however, are allocated to either the urban service districts or the county-wide district. As a result of these allocations, and the general structure of government in the state, the Council will, in fact, be less than totally free to make and change allocations.

All functions now performed by Mecklenburg County on a county-wide basis will continue as county-wide functions. A number of functions now provided by both governments—fire protection, police protection, refuse collection and disposal—will probably be provided at a higher level within urban service districts. All street-aid revenues are allocated to urban service districts. Because of this fact, and because the state and cities now share responsibility for streets, all street functions will be provided only in urban service districts.

If all seven governments were merged, the Charter Commission estimates that of the 1970–71 budgeted expenditures of $100.9 million, $75.2 million would have been allocated county-wide under the plan of consolidation and $25.7 million would have represented expenditures of the urban service districts. Included in the county-wide part of the budget in this analysis are expenditures for water and sewerage and airports (self-supporting), all refuse disposal, all hospital and library expenditures, and about half of the law enforcement expenditures. The major allocations to the urban service districts were all street and street-related functions, garbage collection, higher levels of fire protection, law enforcement and recreation, and model cities. Expenditure allocations carry with them all outlays for operations, maintenance, capital outlay, and debt service.

Some revenues are allocated according to expenditures—fees and charges associated with a function. The local sales tax revenues and earnings from the ABC system are left to the Council to allocate. As a result, it is impossible to indicate precisely the impact of consolidation. The Council could make allocations of expenditures and revenues so as to result in almost no change for any existing taxpayer, regardless of where he resides. However, if the sales and ABC revenues are distributed as they are now distributed between city and county governments, and if the Council thinks the above allocations of expenditures to be reasonable, taxpayers within the cities will have a net

tax decrease and those in the unincorporated areas of the county a slight increase as the result of consolidation.

Tax Limitations. The plan provides for a property tax limit of $1.50 in urban service districts, exclusive of taxes for debt service or those specially voted by the people. The county-wide limitation is $.75 on the $100 valuation, exclusive of taxes for schools, debt service, or specially voted levies.

Borrowing. All bonds issued in the future will be issued by the consolidated government even though the proceeds may be used for a purpose that, at the time of issue, is provided only in an urban service district. In this latter case, however, if the bonds are voted on by the people, they will require majorities in the urban service districts as well as in the county-wide vote.

Planning. Special efforts were made to strengthen the role of planning. The charter requires both a comprehensive plan for the county and long-range capital improvement planning. And all capital construction, acquisition or disposition of land, or change in the use of land by any public agency must be approved in advance by the planning director as being in conformity with the comprehensive plan. Only the Council may overrule a disapproval by the planning director.

Budgeting. The budgeting procedure follows generally that currently existing for cities and counties in North Carolina, except that a requirement for a public hearing before adoption has been added.

Representation. In addition to specific requirements in particular cases, the charter requires that in making appointments to all boards, commissions, and committees the Council shall secure reasonable representation of all "sexes, races, income groups, geographic sections of the county and political parties," reflecting the general thrust of the plan toward assuring representative government.

Transition

The concept of two service districts, with one being a subordinate taxing area, will not become possible under the North Carolina Constitution until July 1, 1973. As a result, the effective date of consolidation was set for August 15, 1972, and the consolidated government is directed to administer the 1972–73 budgets adopted by the various governments just before merger in accordance with their terms. Thus the first consolidated budget, using the service districts, will be the 1973–74 budget.

Special elections for the first members of the Council and for mayor will be held in the spring

New Books in the Institute Library

American Automobile Association. *Digest of Motor Laws.* Washington: American Automobile Association, 1971. Gift.

Bassiouni, M. Cherif. *Criminal Law and Its Processes; the Law of Public Order.* Springfield, Ill.: Charles C. Thomas, 1970. $14.50.

Black, Perry, ed. *Drugs and the Brain; Papers on the Action, Use and Abuse of Psychotropic Agents.* Baltimore: Johns Hopkins Press, 1949. $10.00.

Christensen, Barlow F. *Lawyers for People of Moderate Means: Some Problems of Availability of Legal Services.* Chicago: American Bar Foundation, 1970. $7.50.

George, B. James. *Constitutional Limitations on Evidence in Criminal Cases.* New York: Practicing Law Institute, 1969. $15.00.

Frank, John Paul. *American Law: the Case for Radical Reform.* New York: Macmillan, 1969.

Golembiewski, Robert. *Sensitivity Training and the Laboratory Approach: Readings about Concepts and Applications.* Itasca, Ill.: F. E. Peacock, 1970.

Heap, Desmond. *An Outline of Planning Law.* 5th ed. London: Sweet and Maxwell, 1969. $6.00.

Karlen, Delmar. *Judicial Administration, the American Experience.* Dobbs Ferry, N. Y.: Oceana Press, 1970. $5.75.

Kress, Paul J. *Social Science and the Idea of Progress, the Ambiguous Legacy of Arthur F. Bentley.* Urbana: University of Illinois Press, 1970.

Kurland, Philip B., ed. *The Supreme Court Review, 1970.* Chicago: University of Chicago Press, 1970.

Lovejoy, Clarence E., ed. *Lovejoy's College Guide.* 11th ed. New York, Simon and Schuster, 1971.

North Carolina. Dept. of Archives and History. *Thirty-third Biennial Report, 1968-70.* Raleigh: 1970. Gift.

Robert, Henry Martyn. *Robert's Rules of Order.* (Newly Revised) New York: Scott Foresman, 1970. $5.95.

Smith, Wallace. *Housing, the Social and Economic Elements.* Berkeley: University of California Press, 1970. $12.95.

Tacheron, Donald. *The Job of the Congressman, an Introduction to Service in the U. S. House of Representatives.* 2nd ed. Indianapolis: Bobbs-Merrill Co., 1970.

Toffler, Alvin. *Future Shock.* Annapolis, Md.: Futremics [1970]. $7.95.

---

of 1973. Thereafter, they will be held in the fall of odd-numbered years.

State Interest

Considerable interest in the proposed plan of consolidation has been evidenced throughout North Carolina. Consolidation is not a new idea for the local governments in the state, but achieving consolidation would give Charlotte and Mecklenburg County a first. Moreover, a number of places have special interest. A charter commission has been working on a consolidation plan for Wilmington and New Hanover County for over six months, and legislation to create a charter com-

mission for Durham and Durham County is under active consideration. A special governmental study group, with functional mergers or eventual full consolidation on its agenda, has been formed in Winston-Salem and Forsyth County, and Fayetteville and Cumberland County have endorsed special legislation to create a local government study group for that area. A dozen other cities and counties have also seen less formal and more limited interest in the possibilities of consolidation.

If Mecklenburg voters approve the consolidation of Charlotte and Mecklenburg County on March 22, it could be the first of a number of city-county consolidations in the state during this decade.

Lightning Source UK Ltd.
Milton Keynes UK
UKHW04f1417250818
327788UK00016B/1627/P